The Good, The Bad, & The Hope We Have

A Treasury of Useful Quotations

Compiled By Larry Vaughn

The Good, The Bad, & The Hope We Have

A Treasury of Useful Quotations

Copyright © 2025 by Larry Vaughn

All rights reserved, including the right to reproduce this book or portions thereof in any form whatsoever.

Scriptures marked KJV are taken from The Holy Bible, King James Version.

Scriptures marked ESV are taken from The Holy Bible, English Standard Version® (ESV®), copyright © 2001 by Crossway, a publishing ministry of Good News Publishers. Used by permission. All rights reserved.

Scriptures marked NCV are taken from the NEW CENTURY VERSION (NCV): Scripture taken from the NEW CENTURY VERSION®. Copyright© 2005 by Thomas Nelson, Inc. Used by permission. All rights reserved.

Scriptures marked CEV are taken from the CONTEMPORARY ENGLISH VERSION (CEV): Scripture taken from the CONTEMPORARY ENGLISH VERSION copyright© 1995 by the American Bible Society. Used by permission.

Scripture quotations marked (GNT) are from the Good News Translation in Today's English Version- Second Edition Copyright © 1992 by American Bible Society. Used by permission.

ISBN: 978-0-9982469-8-7
ISBN: 978-0-9982469-9-4 (eBook)

Contents

Introduction

Part One: The Good
    The Abolition of Slavery in America
    God-Fearing American Patriots:
        John Adams
        Samuel Adams
        Benjamin Franklin
        Thomas Jefferson
        George Washington
        James Madison
        Alexander Hamilton
        Noah Webster
        Abraham Lincoln
        John F. Kennedy
        Ronald Reagan
    Everyone In America Needs to Know These Things

Part Two: The Bad
    A. Wolves in Sheep's Clothing
        Marxist University Professors
        Marxist Community Organizers
        Propagandists
        The Mockingbird Media
        Propagandizing The American People
        Why Do They Continue to Lie?
        God-Hating Anti-Americans:
        Karl Marx
        Vladimir Lenin
        Joseph Stalin
        Mao Zedong
        Adolph Hitler
        Joseph Goebbels
        Fidel Castro

   B. The American Marxists' Agenda
- Dethroning God
- Abolishing The Truth
- Capturing Our Children
- Abolishing Education
- Abolishing The Nuclear Family
- Abolishing Freedom of Speech
- Abolishing Freedom of Religion
- Destroying The Bible
- Destroying Christianity
- Abolishing Morality
- Ignoring The Constitution
- Abolishing The Rule of Law
- Confiscating All Guns and Ammunition
- Confiscating All Our Assets
- Destroying The American Middle Class
- The American Marxists' Big Lie
- The False Gospel of Wokeism
- The Goal of Socialism Is Communism

Part Three: The Hope We Have
- The Weapons of Our Warfare:
- Knowing The Truth
- Speaking The Truth
- Having Faith in God
- Doing What's Right
- Praying Every Day
- Using Our God-Given Gifts
- Informing As Many People as Possible

Conclusion

This Is Our Mission

Introduction

Once again, as it was in Lincoln's day, we are a nation divided against itself. We're divided into two groups of people with two different mindsets and two different philosophies of life — individualists and collectivists.

Most Americans are individualists. We're the spiritual descendants of God-fearing patriots such as George Washington, John Adams, and Thomas Jefferson. We believe in God-given rights to life, liberty, and property.

Collectivists are followers of God-hating anti-Americans, such as Marx, Lenin, Stalin, Hitler, and Mao Zedong. Since they didn't believe in God, they didn't believe in God-given rights. Essentially, there is no difference between socialism, communism, Marxism, fascism, and Nazism. They are merely different varieties of collectivism.

We the People of the United States are engaged in a great civil war. It's not merely a war between liberals and conservatives or Democrats and Republicans. It's truly a war between good and evil. William F. Buckley, Jr. described it like this. He said,

1. "The duel between Christianity and atheism is the most important in the world."

He also explicitly equated that conflict with the one between individualism and collectivism.

We are at a critical juncture because the war is escalating rapidly, and things are getting ugly. The Marxists are trying to destroy capitalism,

Christianity, and the Constitution. And the American Patriots are trying to preserve them. We are in the same situation as we were when Abraham Lincoln said,

2. "A house divided against itself cannot stand." I believe this government cannot endure, permanently half slave and half free. I do not expect the Union to be dissolved - I do not expect the house to fall - but I do expect it will cease to be divided. It will become all one thing, or all the other."

The Good, The Bad, & The Hope We Have presents quotations from the thought leaders of both groups. Compare and contrast what these men have said and decide for yourself which side you want to be on in this war.

How do we know the good guys from the bad guys? The Bible tells us:

3. "A good man out of the good treasure of his heart bringeth forth that which is good; and an evil man out of the evil treasure of his heart bringeth forth that which is evil: for of the abundance of the heart his mouth speaketh."

Karl Marx and Vladimir Lenin were the founding fathers of communism, and these are its guiding principles.

Karl Marx said:

4. "There are, besides, eternal truths, such as Freedom, etc., that are common to all states of society. But Communism abolishes eternal truths, it abolishes all religion, and all morality, instead of constituting them on a new basis; it therefore acts in contradiction to all past historical experience."

Vladimir Lenin said:

5. "Dictatorship is rule based directly upon force and unrestricted by any laws. The revolutionary dictatorship of the proletariat is rule won and

maintained by the use of violence by the proletariat against the bourgeoisie, rule that is unrestricted by any laws."

Progressive educator John Dewey was called the Father of Modern Education. He was so impressed with the Soviet Union's education system that he changed ours to be like it. Both were based on the following false assumptions:

6. *"Faith in the prayer-hearing God is an unproved and outmoded faith. There is no god and there is no soul. Hence, there is no need for the props of traditional religion. With dogma and creed excluded, the immutable truth is dead and buried. There is no room for fixed or natural law or permanent moral absolutes."*

Noah Webster was called the Father of American Scholarship and Education. He was an educator, a historian, and a textbook author. He helped with the wording of the United States Constitution. This quotation is from his American Dictionary of the English Language:

7. *"Every civil government is based upon some religion or philosophy of life. Education in a nation will propagate the religion of that nation. In America, the foundational religion was Christianity. It was sown in the hearts of Americans through the home, private, and public schools for centuries.*

"Our liberty, growth, and prosperity was the result of a Biblical philosophy of life. Our continued freedom and success is dependent on our educating the youth of America in the principles of Christianity."

At the present time, there are two revolutions going on in America—the American Revolution and the Communist Revolution. That's why we Americans are so divided. The Marxists want to transform America into a communist nation like Venezuela, and the American patriots will never let that happen.

This was John Adams' explanation of the American Revolution:

8. "But what do We mean by the American Revolution? Do We mean the American War? The Revolution was effected before the War commenced. The Revolution was in the Minds and Hearts of the People. A Change in their Religious Sentiments of their Duties and Obligations."

This was Karl Marx's explanation of the Communist Revolution:

9. "The Communists disdain to conceal their views and aims. They openly declare that their ends can be attained only by the forcible overthrow of all existing social conditions. Let the ruling classes tremble at a Communistic revolution. The proletarians have nothing to lose but their chains. They have a world to win. Workers of the world, unite!"

The United States of America is a constitutional republic. And this experiment in self-government has lasted for two hundred and fifty years. Ronald Reagan explained how it works:

10. "Ours was the first revolution in the history of mankind that truly reversed the course of government, and with three little words: 'We the People.' 'We the People' tell the government what to do; it doesn't tell us. 'We the People' are the driver; the government is the car. And we decide where it should go, and by what route, and how fast.

"Almost all the world's constitutions are documents in which governments tell the people what their privileges are. Our Constitution is a document in which 'We the People' tell the government what it is allowed to do. 'We the People' are free."

The American form of government, as Abraham Lincoln explained, is a government of the people, by the people and for the people. And Thomas Jefferson was right when he said,

11. "Wherever the people are well informed they can be trusted with their own government; that whenever things get so far wrong as to attract their notice, they may be relied on to set them to rights."

"The good sense of the people will always be found to be the best army. They may be led astray for a moment, but will soon correct themselves."

So, the American Revolution has never actually ended. It's still going on in the hearts and minds of the American people, and we will never surrender our liberty and freedom.

Part One: The Good

The Pilgrims came to the New World in 1620 to worship God according to the dictates of their conscience. They suffered incredible hardships. Half of them died the first year. They paved the way for the Puritans, who came here ten years later.

The Puritans were devout Christians who wanted to spread the light of the Gospel to North America. They made a covenant with God and each other to follow God's two great commandments — to love God with all their hearts and minds, and to love their neighbors as themselves. No other nation had done that since the Children of Israel entered the Promised Land.

They wanted to show the world what happens when people honor God and keep his word. "We shall be as a shining city set upon a hill," they said.

The Puritans sold their surplus corn to the British, and their governor let everyone keep the money they earned. This was the beginning of free market capitalism in the Massachusetts Bay Colony, and it was a large contributing factor to the Great Puritan Migration.

Between 1630 and 1638, twenty thousand more Puritans came from England and joined their brethren. These people and their descendants created our unique American culture — a culture based on liberty and freedom and the morality established by the Bible.

America was, and still is, the shining city on a hill. We are the freest and most prosperous nation the world has ever seen. And it's all because of the blessing of Almighty God.

As the population of the colonies increased and the people prospered, they forgot about God. Then, in 1746, The Great Awakening began. During the Great Awakening, the colonists developed a renewed interest in Christianity. It started in the church of Jonathan Edwards in Northampton, Massachusetts.

This Christian revival movement spread like wildfire throughout the colonies through the preaching of George Whitefield.

Whitefield was a preacher from England who perfected the art of open-air preaching. According to Benjamin Franklin, Whitefield could be heard by thirty thousand people at once. He traveled extensively throughout the colonies, preaching the Good News of Jesus Christ. During the Great Awakening, the Baptist, Methodist, and Presbyterian churches enjoyed tremendous increases in membership.

King George III was oppressing the American colonists by demanding more and more of their money. The thirteen English colonies rebelled against King George and declared their independence from Great Britain on July 4, 1776.

King George commanded the most powerful military force in the world, and he sent his army to quell this rebellion. The colonists had to either surrender their freedom or fight for it, and they decided to fight.

We know the signers of the Declaration of Independence were God-fearing men because of what they said in it. They said:

12. *"We are endowed by our Creator with certain unalienable rights, among them are life, liberty and the pursuit of happiness."* ...

"And for the support of this Declaration, with a firm Reliance on the Protection of divine Providence, we mutually pledge to each other our Lives, our Fortunes, and our sacred Honor."

George Washington took a group of untrained civilians and defeated the most powerful military force on earth. How in the world did that happen?

It was because of the intervention of Almighty God, as the Bible says:

13. "For the Lord your God is he who goes with you to fight for you against your enemies, to give you the victory."

Dr. Benjamin Rush was the youngest signer of the Declaration of Independence. He said,

14. "The American war is over; but this is far from being the case with the American revolution. On the contrary, nothing but the first act of the drama is closed. It remains yet to establish and perfect our new forms of government, and to prepare the principles, morals, and manners of our citizens for these forms of government after they are established and brought to perfection."

Our victory over the British was certainly a miracle of God. Then, God performed another miracle by giving us The United States Constitution. Benjamin Rush also said,

15. "I do not believe that the Constitution was the offspring of inspiration, but I am as perfectly satisfied that the Union of the United States in its form and adoption is as much the work of a Divine Providence as any of the miracles recorded in the Old and New Testament."

The Abolition of Slavery in America

The First Great Awakening ignited the American Revolution, and the Second Great Awakening set the stage for the abolition of slavery in America.

The Second Great Awakening was a Christian revival movement that started in 1795 and continued until 1835. One of its leaders was Timothy Dwight. Dr. Dwight was the grandson of Jonathan Edwards, and he was president of Yale College from 1795 until 1817.

Charles G. Finney was another leader of the Second Great Awakening. He is credited with converting five-hundred thousand people to Christianity. He was a strong abolitionist who urged his followers to take part in the anti-slavery movement. And those Christians put an end to slavery in America.

Abolitionists formed the Republican Party in Ripon, Wisconsin, in 1854. Abraham Lincoln was their first candidate for President of the United States, and the American people elected him President in 1860.

The Civil War began in 1861 and ended in 1865. The most popular song among the Union soldiers was *The Battle Hymn of the Republic*. Here are two of the verses:

16. "I have read a fiery gospel writ in burnish'd rows of steel:
"As ye deal with my condemners so with you my grace shall deal;
Let the Hero, born of woman, crush the serpent with his heel,
Since God is marching on." ...

In the beauty of the lilies, Christ was born across the sea,
With a glory in his bosom that transfigures you and me:

As he died to make men holy, let us die to make men free,
While God is marching on."

Six hundred thousand men died in the struggle to end slavery in America. Most of them were white men. And that is exactly what they did—they died to make men free.

Abraham Lincoln issued the Emancipation Proclamation on January 1, 1863. It said that "all persons held as slaves" within the rebellious states "are, and henceforward shall be free."

After the war, Congress enacted the Thirteenth, Fourteenth, and Fifteenth Amendments to the Constitution. The Thirteenth Amendment says:

17. "Neither slavery nor involuntary servitude, except as a punishment for crime whereof the party shall have been duly convicted, shall exist within the United States, or any place subject to their jurisdiction."

The Fourteenth Amendment says:

18. "No state may make or enforce any law which shall abridge the privileges or immunities of citizens of the United States; nor shall any State deprive any person of life, liberty, or property, without due process of law; nor deny to any person within its jurisdiction the equal protection of law."

The Fifteenth Amendment says:

19. "The right of citizens of the United States to vote shall not be denied or abridged by the United States or by any State on account of race, color, or previous condition of servitude."

A hundred years later, at the March on Washington in 1963, Reverend Martin Luther King, Jr. challenged the United States government to live up to the principles stated in the Constitution. And to put an end to discrimination against the black citizens of the United States.

Congress responded to this challenge by passing the Civil Rights Act of 1964 and the Voting Rights Act of 1965. These laws made it illegal to discriminate against anyone based on race, sex, color, religion, or national origin. Or, to prevent them from voting.

God-Fearing American Patriots

John Adams was the second President of the United States. He signed the Declaration of Independence and the Constitution. He negotiated the treaty with the British which ended the Revolutionary War. Here are some of his best quotes:

20. "Liberty cannot be preserved without general knowledge among the people."

21. "The moment the idea is admitted into society, that property is not as sacred as the laws of God, and that there is not a force of law and public justice to protect it, anarchy and tyranny commence."

22. "I now believe, that those general principles of Christianity are as eternal and immutable as the existence and attributes of God."

23. "Every measure of prudence, therefore, ought to be assumed for the eventual total extirpation of slavery from the United States... I have, throughout my whole life, held the practice of slavery in... abhorrence."

Samuel Adams was called the Father of the American Revolution. He was a founding member of the Sons of Liberty. He organized the Boston Tea Party and signed the Declaration of Independence. Here are some of his best quotes:

24. "The Legislative has no right to absolute, arbitrary power over the lives and fortunes of the people; nor can mortals assume a prerogative not only too high for men, but for angels, and therefore reserved for the exercise of the Deity alone."

25. "What a man has honestly acquired is absolutely his own, which he may freely give but cannot be taken from him without his consent."

26. *"Now what liberty can there be, where property is taken away without consent?"*

27. *"If ever the Time should come, when vain & aspiring Men shall possess the highest Seats in Government, our Country will stand in Need of its experienced Patriots to prevent its Ruin."*

28. *"Courage, then, my countrymen, our contest is not only whether we ourselves shall be free, but whether there shall be left to mankind an asylum on earth for civil and religious liberty."*

Benjamin Franklin was a statesman, diplomat, inventor, and scientist. He signed both the Declaration of Independence and the Constitution. He persuaded the French to fight with us against the British in the Revolutionary War. He founded the University of Pennsylvania. Here are some of his best quotes:

29. *"A nation of well-informed men who have been taught to know and prize the rights which God has given them cannot be enslaved. It is in the region of ignorance that tyranny begins."*

30. *"Let me, then, not fail to praise my God continually, for it is his due, and it is all I can return for his many favors and great goodness to me; and let me resolve to be virtuous, that I may be happy, that I may please him who is delighted to see me happy."*

31. *"An external tax is a duty laid on commodities imported; that duty is added to the first cost, and when it is offered to sale, makes a part of the price. If the people don't like it at that price, they refuse it; they are not obliged to pay it. But an internal tax is forced upon the people without their consent, if not laid by their own representatives."*

32. *"The Stamp Act says, we shall have no commerce, make no exchange of property with each other, neither purchase nor grant, nor recover debts; we shall neither marry nor make our wills, unless we pay such

sums, and thus it is intended to extort our money from us, or ruin us by the consequences of refusing to pay for it."

Thomas Jefferson was the principal author of the Declaration of Independence and the third President of the United States. He founded the University of Virginia. Here are some of his best quotes:

33. "The God who gave us life gave us liberty at the same time; the hand of force may destroy but cannot disjoin them."

34. "The voluntary support of laws, formed by persons of their own choice, distinguishes peculiarly the minds capable of self-government. The contrary spirit is anarchy, which of necessity produces despotism."

35. "If we can but prevent the government from wasting the labors of the people, under the pretense of taking care of them, they must become happy."

36. "To compel a man to subsidize with his taxes the propagation of ideas which he disbelieves and abhors is sinful and tyrannical."

George Washington was the Father of Our Country and the first President of the United States. He defeated the British in the Revolutionary War. He could have been the King of America. But he chose to be President for two four-year terms instead. He was first in war, first in peace, and first in the hearts of his countrymen. He said:

37. "Let us therefore rely upon the goodness of the Cause, and the aid of the supreme Being, in whose hands Victory is, to animate and encourage us to great and noble Actions—The Eyes of all our Countrymen are now upon us, and we shall have their blessings, and praises, if happily we are the instruments of saving them from the Tyranny meditated against them.

"Let us therefore animate and encourage each other, and shew the whole world, that a Freeman contending for Liberty on his own ground is superior to any slavish mercenary on earth."

38. *"The hour is fast approaching, on which the Honor and Success of this army, and the safety of our bleeding Country depend. Remember officers and Soldiers, that you are Freemen, fighting for the blessings of Liberty that slavery will be your portion, and that of your posterity, if you do not acquit yourselves like men."*

39. *"Since we ought to be no less persuaded that the propitious smiles of heaven, can never be expected on a nation that disregards the eternal rules of order and right, which heaven itself has ordained.*

"And since the preservation of the sacred fire of liberty, and the destiny of the republican model of government, are justly considered as deeply, perhaps as finally staked on the experiment entrusted to the hands of the American people."

James Madison was the fourth President of the United States. He was the Father of the Constitution and the principal author of the Bill of Rights. He said:

40. *"In the former sense, a man's land, or merchandise, or money is called his property. In the latter sense, a man has a property in his opinions and the free communication of them. He has a property of peculiar value in his religious opinions, and in the profession and practice dictated by them.*

"He has a property very dear to him in the safety and liberty of his person. He has an equal property in the free use of his faculties and free choice of the objects on which to employ them.

"In a word, as a man is said to have a right to his property, he may be equally said to have a property in his rights. Where an excess of power prevails, property of no sort is duly respected. No man is safe in his opinions, his person, his faculties, or his possessions."

41. *"Government is instituted to protect property of every sort; as well that which lies in the various rights of individuals, as that which the term*

particularly expresses. This being the end of government, that alone is a just government, which impartially secures to every man, whatever is his own."

42. "A just security to property is not afforded by that government, under which unequal taxes oppress one species of property and reward another species."

Alexander Hamilton was George Washington's right-hand man during the Revolutionary War. He was instrumental in the defeat of the British at Yorktown, and he was the first Secretary of the Treasury. He said:

43. "The sacred rights of mankind are not to be rummaged for, among old parchments, or musty records. They are written, as with a sun beam, in the whole volume of human nature, by the hand of the divinity itself; and can never be erased or obscured by mortal power."

44. "Here sir, the people govern; here they act by their immediate representatives."

45. "It was certainly true that nothing like an equality of property existed: that an inequality would exist as long as liberty existed, and that it would unavoidably result from that very liberty itself."

46. "The fundamental source of all your errors, sophisms and false reasonings is a total ignorance of the natural rights of mankind. Were you once to become acquainted with these, you could never entertain a thought, that all men are not, by nature, entitled to a parity of privileges.

"You would be convinced, that natural liberty is a gift of the beneficent Creator to the whole human race, and that civil liberty is founded in that; and cannot be wrested from any people, without the most manifest violation of justice."

Noah Webster was an educator and a textbook author, who was known as The Schoolmaster of the Republic. He said:

47. *"The Bible must be considered as the great source of all the truth by which men are to be guided in government as well as in all social transactions."*

48. *"When you become entitled to exercise the right of voting for public officers, let it be impressed on your mind that God commands you to choose for rulers, 'just men who will rule in the fear of God.'*

"The preservation of government depends on the faithful discharge of this duty; if the citizens neglect their duty and place unprincipled men in office, the government will soon be corrupted; laws will be made, not for the public good so much as for selfish or local purposes; corrupt or incompetent men will be appointed to execute the laws; the public revenues will be squandered on unworthy men; and the rights of the citizens will be violated or disregarded.

"If a republican government fails to secure public prosperity and happiness, it must be because the citizens neglect the divine commands, and elect bad men to make and administer the laws."

Abraham Lincoln was the sixteenth President of the United States. He had two significant accomplishments. He preserved the Union, and he put an end to slavery in America.

He gave his most famous speech shortly after the Battle of Gettysburg on November 19, 1863. The Gettysburg Address is one of the greatest speeches of all time, and this is it in its entirety:

49. *"Four score and seven years ago our fathers brought forth, on this continent, a new nation, conceived in Liberty, and dedicated to the proposition that all men are created equal.*

Now we are engaged in a great civil war, testing whether that nation, or any nation so conceived and so dedicated, can long endure. We are met on a great battle-field of that war. We have come to dedicate a portion of that field, as a final resting place for those who here gave their lives that that nation might live. It is altogether fitting and proper that we should do this.

But, in a larger sense, we can not dedicate—we can not consecrate—we can not hallow—this ground. The brave men, living and dead, who struggled here, have consecrated it, far above our poor power to add or detract. The world will little note, nor long remember what we say here, but it can never forget what they did here. It is for us the living, rather, to be dedicated here to the unfinished work which they who fought here have thus far so nobly advanced.

It is rather for us to be here dedicated to the great task remaining before us—that from these honored dead we take increased devotion to that cause for which they gave the last full measure of devotion—that we here highly resolve that these dead shall not have died in vain—that this nation, under God, shall have a new birth of freedom—and that government of the people, by the people, for the people, shall not perish from the earth."

John F. Kennedy was the thirty-fifth President of the United States. He was the youngest man ever elected President, and he was assassinated in 1963. These quotes are from his inaugural address:

50. *"The cost of freedom is always high, but Americans have always paid it. And one path we shall never choose, and that is the path of surrender or submission."*

51. *"Let the word go forth from this time and place, to friend and foe alike, that the torch has been passed to a new generation of Americans, born in this century, tempered by war, disciplined by a hard and bitter peace, proud of our ancient heritage, and unwilling to witness or permit the slow undoing of those human rights to which this nation has always been committed, and to which we are committed today at home and around the world."*

52. *"Let every nation know, whether it wishes us well or ill, that we shall pay any price, bear any burden, meet any hardship, support any friend, oppose any foe to assure the survival and the success of liberty."*

Ronald Reagan was the fortieth President of the United States. He defeated the Soviet Union in the Cold War. Here are some of his best quotes:

53. "How do you tell a Communist? Well, it's someone who reads Marx and Lenin. And how do you tell an anti-Communist? It's someone who understands Marx and Lenin."

54. "Government's first duty is to protect the people, not run their lives."

55. "I hope that we once again have reminded people that man is not free unless the government is limited. There's a clear cause and effect here that is as neat and predictable as a law of physics: As government expands, liberty contracts."

56. "If we lose freedom here, there's no place to escape to. This is the last stand on earth."

Everyone In America Needs to Know These Things

The war we are in isn't anything new. It's a continuation of the age-old conflict between good and evil, and the struggle to be free from the oppression of a tyrannical government.

Samuel Adams said,

57. *"The natural liberty of man is to be free from any superior power on Earth, and not to be under the will or legislative authority of man, but only to have the law of nature for his rule."*

John F. Kennedy said,

58. *"The greatest revolution in the history of man, past, present and future, is the revolution of those determined to be free."*

59. *"And yet the same revolutionary belief for which our forebears fought is still at issue around the globe, the belief that the rights of man come not from the generosity of the state but from the hand of God."*

The American Revolution is still going on in the hearts and minds of today's American patriots. And we agree:

60. *"We shall pay any price, bear any burden, meet any hardship, support any friend, oppose any foe to assure the survival and the success of liberty."*

And this is our prayer:

61. *"That this nation, under God, shall have a new birth of freedom - and that government of the people, by the people, for the people, shall not perish from the earth."*

Part Two: The Bad

A. Wolves in Sheep's Clothing

The American Marxists call themselves liberals, progressives, and democratic socialists. They don't mind being called leftists. But they don't think of themselves as communists, even though they're following the teachings of Karl Marx, which is Communism.

62. "To a considerable extent, without knowing it, many people are philosophical Marxists, although they use different names for their philosophical ideas."—Ludwig von Mises

There are two kinds of communists: Marxist-Leninists and Fabian Socialists. Marxist-Leninists, like Fidel Castro, use violence to seize power, while Fabian Socialists use stealth and deception.

The Fabian Society was founded in London in 1884. It was named after Quintus Fabius, the Roman general who defeated his enemies gradually over long periods of time. Aldous Huxley, George Orwell, H. G. Wells, George Bernard Shaw, and John Maynard Keynes were Fabian Socialists. John Dewey was an American Fabian Socialist.

The Fabian Society's coat of arms is a wolf in sheep's clothing. One version of their flag has the following inscription on it:

63. "For the right moment you must wait, as Fabius did most patiently, when warring against Hannibal, though many censured his delays; but when the time comes you must strike hard, as Fabius did, or your waiting will be in vain, and fruitless."

Fabian Socialists are also known as Democratic Socialists. Their logo, the tortoise, reminds them that "slow and steady wins the race." They've been racing to destroy America for over a hundred years. They intend to steal everything we have — our freedom, our children, and our private property, and to make us slaves of a socialist state.

U. S. Senator Bernie Sanders calls himself a Democratic Socialist as does Zohran Mamdani. Alexandria Ocasio-Cortez and Rashida Tlaib are members of the Democratic Socialists of America and members of the U. S. House of Representatives.

The Communist Manifesto is the American Marxists' Bible, and Marx and Lenin are their prophets. They've usurped the authority of "We the People" as the rightful government of the United States. And they're imposing their political philosophy of communism on the rest of us.

Marxists believe that capitalism is the root of all evil. They think it's unfair for one person to have more than anyone else. So, they want to confiscate all private property and make everyone a pauper.

They are trying to destroy our unique American culture. And they've been working toward that goal for decades using a strategy devised by Antonio Gramsci.

Antonio Gramsci was a leader in the Italian Communist Party. He is known as the Godfather of Cultural Marxism. It was his idea to capture our culture by infiltrating our universities, our media, and our government. He said,

64. *"Socialism is precisely the religion that must overwhelm Christianity... In the new order, Socialism will triumph by first capturing the culture via infiltration of schools, universities, churches, and the media by transforming the consciousness of society."*

Joseph Buttigieg was a professor of English at Notre Dame University. He edited the English version of Gramsci's *Prison Diaries* and was president of the International Gramsci Society. Incidentally, he was also the father of Pete Buttigieg. Pete Buttigieg was a candidate for President in 2020.

American Marxists have adopted the political philosophy of the Frankfurt School, known as Critical Theory. The Frankfurt School was a group of Marxist intellectuals from Frankfurt, Germany. They set out to destroy capitalism, Christianity, the nuclear family, and everything else that's associated with Western Civilization.

Max Horkheimer was one of the leaders of the Frankfurt School and a proponent of Critical Theory. He agreed with Antonio Gramsci on the best way of converting Americans to Marxism: To infiltrate America's universities, media, and government agencies and transform them into Marxist entities. To capture the hearts and minds of America's young people, and to transform the consciousness of society.

Max Horkheimer and other members of the Frankfurt School moved to the United States in 1935. They infiltrated Columbia University first and then moved on to Harvard. Derrick Bell was the first black law professor at Harvard. Classical Marxism was about the poor being oppressed by the rich. But it was Derrick Bell's idea for the American version of Marxism to be about the blacks being oppressed by the whites. And that was the beginning of Critical Race Theory.

Max Horkheimer, Theodor Adorno, and Herbert Marcuse set up a second Marxist enclave in California. Horkheimer and Adorno returned to Germany, but Marcuse stayed behind. He became a professor of philosophy at the University of California, San Diego. He indoctrinated thousands of his students into Marxism, and he became known as the Father of the New Left.

Herbert Marcuse was best known for creating the doctrine of Liberating Tolerance. Liberating Tolerance is based on the idea that Marxism is objectively true and everything that opposes it is false.

Liberating Tolerance is simply promoting all ideas that come from the Left and suppressing all ideas that come from the Right. So Liberating Tolerance is actually intolerance.

According to Marcuse, this intolerance is justified because it suppresses capitalism. And it must continue until everyone comes to the knowledge of the "truth" of Marxism. That's why Marxists don't allow anyone who disagrees with them to speak freely.

So, the idea of being Woke to Marxism, the suppression of free speech, and the Cancel Culture all started with this Orwellian idea that intolerance is tolerance.

American Marxist college professors have poisoned the well of education in America. They've created an army of political activists who hate God, hate America, and hate everyone who disagrees with them.

They are leaders in academia, media, business, and government throughout America. Some of them are true believers in Marxism, others are useful idiots. They're working together to follow Antonio Gramsci's plan to destroy America. He said:

65. *"The civilized world has been thoroughly saturated with Christianity for 2000 years. Any country grounded in Judeo-Christian values cannot be overthrown until the roots are cut. But to cut the roots - to change culture - a long march through the institutions is necessary. Only then will power fall into our hands like a ripened fruit."*

Marxist College Professors

Angela Davis was a student of Herbert Marcuse, and a professor at the University of California, Santa Cruz. She was associated with the

Black Panther Party. She was the Communist Party USA's candidate for Vice-President of the United States in 1980 and 1984.

Davis was one of the founders of Critical Resistance, an organization that seeks to dismantle the United States prison system. She is presently working with other Marxists to achieve that goal.

Richard Delago and his wife Jean Stefanic are law professors at the University of Alabama. They are co-authors of the book *Critical Race Theory*, the definitive work on the subject. Critical Race Theory has spread, like cancer, to nearly every school, college, and university in America.

Ibram X. Kendi is a professor at Boston University. He is the author of *How to Be an Antiracist*. It became a textbook for the woke generation and a training manual for corporate America and government agencies, including our armed forces. And compliance with its principles was mandatory.

According to Kendi, everyone in America is either a racist or an antiracist. There is no middle ground. He also said the only cure for racial discrimination is for the antiracists to discriminate against the racists.

Robin DiAngelo is a professor at the University of Washington. She is the author of *White Fragility: Why It's So Hard to Talk to White People About Racism*, in which she contends that all white people are racists. This is another instruction manual for our school children. And it's being taught as if it were true.

Nikole Hannah-Jones is a professor of journalism at Howard University. She received a Pulitzer Prize for her book, *The 1619 Project: A New Origin Story*. In this book, Hannah-Jones presents an alternate version of American history.

She claims America began in 1619 when seven African slaves arrived in Jamestown. And the purpose of the Revolutionary War was to preserve the institution of slavery. Legitimate historians have refuted these claims.

But *The 1619 Project* is still being taught in schools throughout America as if it were true.

Marxist Community Organizers

The social justice warriors of America are transforming our nation into a socialist country. And they're being led by professional community organizers who are followers of Saul Alinsky.

Saul Alinsky was a Marxist community organizer in Chicago. His book, *Rules for Radicals*, is an instruction manual for American Marxists. Hillary Clinton was an admirer of Alinsky. Barack Obama followed in his footsteps by becoming a community organizer in Chicago.

Eric Mann was a student of Herbert Marcuse. He is the director of the Labor/Community Strategy Center in Los Angeles. He founded the Students for a Democratic Society (SDS). The mission of the SDS was to promote social change. He was also associated with the Congress of Racial Equality (CORE) and the Black Panther Party.

The Black Panther Party was a communist organization that advocated the violent overthrow of the United States government. In 1967, the Black Panther Party published a ten-point list of their demands. Here is one of them:

66. "We want freedom for all Black men held in federal, state, county … prisons and jails."

Bill Ayers and his wife Bernardine Dohrn founded the Weather Underground, a splinter group of Students for a Democratic Society. The Weather Underground called for the violent overthrow of the United States government and the establishment of a socialist dictatorship.

The Weather Underground claimed credit for twenty-five bombings. They bombed the US Capitol, the Pentagon. The US State Department, the California Attorney General's office and a New York City police station. In 1970, several members of the Weather Underground were placed on the FBI's most wanted list.

Bernardine Dohrn served time in prison, but her husband, Bill Ayers, went free. He became a professor of education at the University of Illinois, where he was an elementary education theorist. Dohrn was a law professor at Northwestern University.

Bill Ayers and Bernardine Dohrn are heroes of the American Marxist community. They launched Barack Obama's political career in the living room of their home in Chicago.

The May 19th Communist Organization (M19CO) was an offshoot of the Weather Underground. May 19th was the birthday of their two favorite revolutionaries, Ho Chi Minh, and Malcolm X. The FBI described the M19CO as "A Marxist-Leninist organization which advocated armed revolution and the violent overthrow of the United States government."

On November 7, 1983, the M19CO exploded a bomb outside the Senate Chamber in the United States Capitol. Susan Rosenberg was a member of M19CO. She was sentenced to fifty-eight years in prison for her terrorist activities. Bill Clinton commuted her sentence on the last day of his presidency.

Susan Rosenberg became a board member of an organization that provided funding for the Black Lives Matter Global Network. She's presently involved in the movement to dismantle the United States prison system.

Richard Cloward and his wife Frances Fox Piven were sociology professors at the Columbia University School of Social Work. They created the Cloward-Piven Strategy, a plan to destroy the American economy by overloading the welfare system.

Patrisse Cullors and Alicia Garcia were two of the founders of Black Lives Matter. Patrice Cullors was the protégé of SDS founder, Eric Mann. She said:

67. "The first thing, I think, is that we actually do have an ideological frame. Myself and Alicia in particular are trained organizers. We are trained Marxists. We are super-versed on, sort of, ideological theories."

Propagandists

68. The Encyclopedia Britannica defines propoganda as "dissemination of information—facts, arguments, rumours, half-truths, or lies—to influence public opinion."

Edward Bernays was the nephew of Sigmund Freud. He pioneered the use of propaganda to control the minds of the masses. He said:

69. "The conscious intelligent manipulation of the organized opinions and habits of the masses is an important element in a democratic society. Those who manipulate this unseen mechanism of society constitute an invisible government which is the true ruling power of our country. We are governed, our minds molded, our tastes formed, our ideas suggested largely by men we have never heard of... It is they who pull the wires that control the public mind."

Joseph Goebbels used Bernays' propaganda techniques to convince the German people that Adolph Hitler would fix their broken economy. And they voted him into power.

The Mockingbird Media

Cultural hegemony is the domination of a people by controlling everything they see, hear, and believe. When people constantly hear the same message from schools, newsrooms, and screens, they will accept it as normal, acceptable, or fact. By guiding the culture, the ruling class controls the beliefs, values and emotions of the masses.

70. Joseph Goebbels said, "It is the absolute right of the state to supervise the formation of public opinion."

71. Vladimir Lenin said, "We must be ready to employ trickery, deceit, law-breaking, withholding and concealing truth. ... We can and must write in a language which sows among the masses hate, revulsion, and scorn toward those who disagree with us."

72. Joseph Stalin said, "The press must grow day in and day out — it is our Party's sharpest and most powerful weapon."

Aleksandr Solzhenitsyn was a Nobel Prize-winning novelist. He spent eight years in a Soviet prison for criticizing Stalin in a personal letter. He was an expert on communist propaganda. He said:

73. "The press has become the greatest power within the Western countries."

Whoever controls the flow of information controls the mind of the masses. In 1950, CIA Director Allen Dulles created Operation Mockingbird. It's a program that allows the CIA to control the information reported to the American people. The Mockingbird Media enables the American Marxists to impose their beliefs on the public mind.

74. In 1975, CIA Director William Colby admitted to Congress, *"The Central Intelligence Agency owns everyone of any significance in the major media."*

75. In 1981, CIA Director William Casey is reported to have said, *"We'll know that our disinformation program is complete when everything the American public believes is false."*

Dr. Joost Meerloo was an expert in the brainwashing techniques of communist governments. They control the flow of information by maintaining absolute control of the narrative. He said:

76. "He who dictates and formulates the words and phrases we use, who is master of the press and radio, is master of the mind. Repeat mechanically your assumptions and suggestions, diminish the opportunity for communicating dissent and opposition. This is the formula for conditioning of the masses."

There is nothing new under the sun. The Founding Fathers were well aware of this tactic. Samuel Adams said,

77. *"How strangely will the Tools of a Tyrant pervert the plain Meaning of Words!"*

John Adams said,

78. *"Abuse of words has been the great instrument of sophistry and chicanery, of party, faction, and division of society."*—John Adams

The American Marxists have used political correctness to commandeer our language and tell us what we can and cannot say. They tell us we must use the term "migrants" instead of "illegal immigrants" and "formerly incarcerated persons" instead of "ex-convicts." Meanwhile, they call everyone who disagrees with them "Fascists" and "Nazis."

Theodore Dalrymple is the pen name of Dr. Anthony Malcomb Daniels. He is a journalist, a psychiatrist, and an expert on communist propaganda. This is his definition of political correctness:

79. *"Political correctness is communist propaganda writ small."*

Propagandizing the American People

The Smith-Mundt Act was a law that prohibited the Federal government from propagandizing the American people. In 2012, Barack Obama signed H. R. 4310, The National Defense Authorization Act. It repealed the Smith-Mundt Act. And now, it's perfectly legal for government officials to tell us outrageous lies.

The United States Agency for Global Media (USAGM) is a U.S. government agency that controls the flow of information on the Internet.

The Open Technology Fund is a non-profit corporation that receives funding from the USAGM and polices the internet.

Vladimir Lenin said,

80. "The press should be not only a collective propagandist and a collective agitator, but also a collective organizer of the masses."

Now, the American mainstream media resembles the news agencies of the Soviet Union. Tass was owned by the Soviet government, and Pravda was the official mouthpiece of the Communist Party. They propagandized the masses by telling them outrageous lies and presenting them as the truth.

Elena Gorokhova described this practice in her novel, *A Mountain of Crumbs*. She said:

81. "The rules are simple: they lie to us, we know they're lying, they know we know they're lying but they keep lying anyway."

Why Do They Continue to Lie?

Because the big lie is their most effective weapon. In his book *Mein Kampf*, Adolph Hitler explained how it works:

82. "In the big lie there is always a certain force of credibility; because the broad masses of a nation are more easily corrupted in the deeper strata of their emotional nature than consciously or voluntarily; and thus in the primitive simplicity of their minds they more readily fall victims to the big lie than to the small lie, since they often tell small lies in little matters but would be ashamed to resort to large scale falsehoods.

"It would never come to their heads to fabricate colossal untruths, and they would not believe that others would have the impudence to distort the truth so infamously."

In his book, *The Rape of the Mind,* Dr. Joost Meerloo described the effects of The Big Lie on the mind of the masses. He called it menticide and this is how he defined it:

83. *"Menticide is an old crime against the human mind and spirit but systematized anew. It is an organized system of psychological intervention and judicial perversion through which a powerful dictator can imprint his own opportunistic thoughts upon the minds of those he plans to use and destroy. The terrorized victims finally find themselves compelled to express complete conformity to the tyrant's wishes."*

84. *"Logic can be met with logic, while illogic cannot—it confuses those who think straight. The Big Lie and monotonously repeated nonsense have more emotional appeal in a cold war than logic and reason. While the enemy is still searching for a reasonable counter-argument to the first lie, the totalitarians can assault him with another."*

Confusing a targeted audience is one of the necessary ingredients for effective mind control.

God-Hating Anti-Americans

Karl Marx created an alternative religion for people who don't believe in God. His followers are expecting to fulfill Marx's utopian fantasy of the "Worker's Paradise." It's a place where there are no nations, no borders, no governments, no police, no crime, no poverty, and no racism—because there is no capitalism. Here are some of his quotes:

85. *"The democratic concept of man is false, because it is Christian. The democratic concept holds that... each man is a sovereign being. This is the illusion, dream, and postulate of Christianity."*

86. *"The first requisite for the happiness of the people is the abolition of religion."*

87. *"In one word, you reproach us with intending to do away with your property. Precisely so, that is just what we intend."*

88. *"Accuse your enemy of what you are doing, as you are doing it to create confusion."*

Vladimir Lenin

Vladimir Lenin was the founder of the Union of Soviet Socialist Republics, the first nation based on Marx's philosophy of government. He was a mass murderer who killed three million of his own people. And an additional forty to sixty million people were murdered before the fall of the Soviet Union in 1991. Here are some of Lenin's quotes:

89. *"The goal of socialism is communism."*

90. *"Soviet power is a new type of state in which there is no bureaucracy, no police, no standing army."*

91. *"People always have been the foolish victims of deception and self-deception in politics, and they always will be, until they have learned to seek out the interests of some class or other behind all moral, religious, political and social phrases, declarations and promises."*

92. *"Hang the kulaks (peasant farmers), execute the hostages. Do it in such a way that people for hundreds of miles away will see and tremble."*

Joseph Stalin

Joseph Stalin succeeded Lenin as the dictator of the Soviet Union. Between 1929 and 1953, he murdered twenty million people. Here are some of his quotes:

93. *"Mankind is divided into rich and poor, into property owners and exploited; and to abstract oneself from this fundamental division, and from the antagonism between poor and rich, means abstracting oneself from fundamental facts."*

94. *"God's not unjust, he doesn't actually exist. We've been deceived. If God existed, he'd have made the world more just..."*

95. *"I consider it completely unimportant who in the party will vote, or how; but what is extraordinarily important is this—who will count the votes, and how."*

Mao Zedong is the man who used communism to conquer China. Forty-five million Chinese people died of state violence, starvation, and overwork during the "Great Leap Forward." Here are some of his quotes:

96. *"We should support whatever the enemy opposes and oppose whatever the enemy supports."*

97. *"Genuine equality between the sexes can only be realized in the process of the socialist transformation of society as a whole."*

98. *"When there is not enough to eat, people starve to death. It is better to let half of the people die so that the other half can eat their fill."*

99. *"A revolution is not a dinner party, or writing an essay, or painting a picture, or doing embroidery; it cannot be so refined, so leisurely and gentle, so temperate, kind, courteous, restrained and magnanimous. A revolution is an insurrection, an act of violence by which one class overthrows another."*

100. *"We are advocates of the abolition of war, we do not want war; but war can only be abolished through war, and in order to get rid of the gun it is necessary to take up the gun."*

101. *"We thank Marx, Engels, Lenin and Stalin for giving us a weapon. This weapon is not a machine gun, but Marxism-Leninism."*

Adolph Hitler was the head of the National Socialist German Workers' Party, also known as the Nazi Party. And he was the

Chancellor of Germany during World War Two. He banned guns in 1938. Then, between 1939 and 1945, he rounded up thirteen million defenseless people and murdered them. Here are some of his quotes:

102. "Basically, National Socialism and Marxism are the same thing."

103. "All propaganda has to be popular and has to adapt its spiritual level to the perception of the least intelligent of those towards whom it intends to direct itself."

104. "The most brilliant propagandist technique will yield no success unless one fundamental principle is borne in mind constantly—it must confine itself to a few points and repeat them over and over."

105. "Only constant repetition will finally succeed in imprinting an idea on the memory of the crowd."

106. "What good fortune for those in power that people do not think."

Joseph Goebbels was Hitler's Minister of Propaganda during World War Two. Here are some of his quotes:

107. "Not every item of news should be published. Rather must those who control news policies endeavor to make every item of news serve a certain purpose."

108. "Whoever can conquer the street will one day conquer the state, for every form of power politics and any dictatorship-run state has its roots in the street."

Fidel Castro used communism to conquer Cuba. He was a mass murderer who killed 150,000 of his own people. Here are some of his quotes:

109. "A revolution is not a bed of roses. A revolution is a struggle to the death between the future and the past."

110. "A revolution is a dictatorship of the exploited against the exploiters."

111. "I am a Marxist-Leninist, and I will be a Marxist-Leninist until the last days of my life."

B. The Marxist Agenda

The American Marxists have completed their long march through the institutions. They've infiltrated our universities, our media, and our government agencies and transformed them into Marxist entities. If they achieve the following goals, then the Communist Revolution in America will be complete. The Revolution is their dream, their quest, and their religion. They don't care about anything else.

Dethroning God

The essence of the Communist Revolution is rebellion against God. It's replacing the truth of God with a lie. It's destroying everything that's good and replacing it with evil.

According to the Bible, the rebellion against God began when Lucifer tried to make himself equal to God. God threw him out of heaven, along with a third of the angels who joined him.

Then, Satan persuaded Adam and Eve to join his rebellion against God. God said, if they ate the forbidden fruit, they would die. Satan told them if they ate it, they would be like God. When they believed Satan's lies, they severed their relationship with God, and they had to leave the Garden of Eden.

When Jesus, the Second Adam, died for our sins and rose from the dead, he restored our relationship with God. He saved us from sin, death, and hell, and he defeated Satan forever.

Even though Satan is a defeated foe, he continues to fight against God and his people. And he's a lot more active lately because he knows his time is short.

In this passage of Scripture, God was addressing Lucifer. He said:

112. "How art thou fallen from heaven, O Lucifer, son of the morning! How art thou cut down to the ground, which didst weaken the nations!

For thou hast said in thine heart, I will ascend into heaven, I will exalt my throne above the stars of God: I will sit also upon the mount of the congregation, in the sides of the north:

I will ascend above the heights of the clouds; I will be like the most High.

Yet thou shalt be brought down to hell, to the sides of the pit."

Karl Marx wasn't an atheist; he was just a man who hated God. And he simply followed the example of his spiritual father, Satan. He said:

113. "I wish to avenge myself against the One who rules above."

Austrian economist Ludwig von Mises accurately described Karl Marx's brand of socialism.

114. "People frequently call socialism a religion. It is indeed the religion of self-deification."

The Patriots' Position:

Evangelist Billy Graham said:

115. "Communism has decided against God, against Christ, against the Bible, and against all religion."

The Anti-Americans' Position:

116. "Faith in the prayer-hearing God is an unproved and outmoded faith. There is no god and there is no soul. Hence, there is no need for the props of traditional religion. With dogma and creed excluded, the immutable truth is dead and buried. There is no room for fixed or natural law or permanent moral absolutes."—John Dewey

Abolishing the Truth

God is the source of all wisdom and truth, and he reveals it to us through the Bible. Light is the symbol of God's word. The psalmist said,

117. "The entrance of thy words giveth light; it giveth understanding unto the simple."

Here, the word "simple" doesn't mean stupid. It means naïve. Knowing God's word makes us wise, so we're not easily deceived, and that's why Jesus said,

118. "If you continue in my word, you will be my disciples indeed, and you will know the truth and the truth will make you free."

Our enemies knew they had to take away our Bibles before they could take away our freedom. Because Horace Greeley was certainly right when he said,

119. "It is impossible to enslave, mentally or socially, a Bible-reading people. The principles of the Bible are the groundwork of human freedom."

The Patriot's Position:

120. "The foundations of our society and our government rest so much on the teachings of the Bible that it would be difficult to support them if faith in these teachings would cease to be practically universal in our country."—Calvin Coolidge

The Anti-Americans' Position:

Karl Marx said:

121. "There are, besides, eternal truths, such as Freedom, Justice, etc., that are common to all states of society. But Communism abolishes eternal truths, it abolishes all religion, and all morality, instead of constituting them on a new basis; it therefore acts in contradiction to all past historical experience."

122. *"In the eyes of dialectical philosophy, nothing is established for all times, nothing is absolute or sacred."*

Capturing Our Children

In Nazi Germany, children were the property of the state. The American Marxists think our children belong to them. They're indoctrinating them into Critical Race Theory and Wokeism. And they're teaching them to hate America, to hate each other, and to hate themselves.

The Patriots' Position:

123. *"But every child in America should be acquainted with his own country. He should read books that furnish him with ideas that will be useful to him in life and practice. As soon as he opens his lips, he should rehearse the history of his own country; he should lisp the praise of liberty, and of those illustrious heroes and statesmen, who have wrought a revolution in her favor."*—Noah Webster

The Anti-Americans' Position:

Adolph Hitler said:

124. *"He alone, who owns the youth, gains the future."*

125. *"When an opponent declares, 'I will not come over to your side,' I calmly say, 'Your child belongs to us already... What are you? You will pass on. Your descendants, however, now stand in the new camp. In a short time they will know nothing else but this new community.'"*

In an address to the Association for Childhood Education International in Denver, CO, in April 1972, Harvard Psychiatrist Chester M. Pierce said:

126. *"Every child in America entering school at the age of five is insane because he comes to school with certain allegiances toward our Founding Fathers, toward his parents, toward belief in a supernatural*

being, toward sovereignty of this nation as a separate entity ... It's up to you [psychiatrists and psychologists] to make these sick children well by creating The International Child of the Future."

Abolishing Education

Noah Webster's *American Dictionary of the English Language* defines education as follows:

127. *"The bringing up, as of a child, instruction; formation of manners. education comprehends all that series of instruction and discipline which is intended to enlighten the understanding, correct the temper, and form the manners and habits of youth, and fit them for usefulness in their future stations.*

"To give children a good education in manners, arts and science, is important; to give them a religious education is indispensable; and an immense responsibility rests on parents and guardians who neglect these duties."

Noah Webster also said,

128. *"Every civil government is based upon some religion or philosophy of life. Education in a nation will propagate the religion of that nation. In America, the foundational religion was Christianity. And it was sown in the hearts of Americans through the home and private and public schools for centuries.*

"Our liberty, growth, and prosperity was the result of a Biblical philosophy of life. Our continued freedom and success is dependent on our educating the youth of America in the principles of Christianity."

129. *"An attempt to conduct the affairs of a free government with wisdom and impartiality, and to preserve the just rights of all classes of citizens, without the guidance of Divine precepts, will certainly end in disappointment.*

"God is the supreme moral Governor of the world He has made, and as He Himself governs with perfect rectitude, He requires His rational creatures to govern themselves in like manner. If men will not submit to be controlled by His laws, He will punish them by the evils resulting from their own disobedience..."

Our education system used to be one of the best in the world. In 1963, the Supreme Court destroyed it when they banned the Bible in our public schools. Now, the Bible is the missing ingredient in our society. And our lack of knowledge of its precepts is destroying us.

Now, we have two generations of Americans with no core values and no moral compass. They're being taught to hate God, hate capitalism, and hate America. And that's the root cause of all the problems we are facing today.

This warning about our colleges and universities has turned out to be prophetic:

130. "I am much afraid that the universities will prove to be the great gates of hell, unless they diligently labour in explaining the Holy Scriptures, and engraving them in the hearts of youth. I advise no one to place his child where the Scriptures do not reign paramount. Every institution in which men are not unceasingly occupied with the Word of God must become corrupt."—Martin Luther

The Patriots' Position:

131. "Educate and inform the whole mass of the people... They are the only sure reliance for the preservation of our liberty."—Thomas Jefferson

132. "The true purpose of education is to prepare young men and women for effective citizenship in a free form of government."—Dwight D. Eisenhower

James Madison said:

133. "Knowledge will forever govern ignorance: And a people who mean to be their own Governors must arm themselves with the power which knowledge gives."

134. "It is universally admitted that a well-instructed people alone can be permanently a free people."

Benjamin Rush said:

135. "The only foundation for a useful education in a republic is to be laid in religion. Without this there can be no virtue, and without virtue there can be no liberty, and liberty is the object and life of all republican governments."

The Anti-Americans' Position:

136. "The education of all children, from the moment that they can get along without a mother's care, shall be in state institutions at state expense."—Karl Marx

137. "Education is a weapon whose effects depend on who holds it in his hands and at whom it is aimed."—Joseph Stalin

138. [Schools should] "take an active part in directing social change and share in the construction of a new social order."—John Dewey

Abolishing the Nuclear Family

God invented marriage, and the purpose of marriage is to create godly offspring. God also invented the family, which is our society's basic building block. And that's why the Marxists are so desperate to destroy them.

139. "Mothers and school-masters plant the seeds of nearly all the good and evil which exists in the world."—Benjamin Rush

The Patriots' Position:

Noah Webster said:

140. "In the family are formed the elements of civil government; the family discipline is the model of all social order; ... the respect for the law and the magistrate begins in the respect for parents... Families are the nurseries of good and bad citizens.

"The parent who neglects to restrain and govern his child, or who, by his example, corrupts him, is the enemy of the community to which he belongs; the parent who instructs his child in good principles, and subjects him to correct discipline, is the guardian angel of his child, and the best benefactor of society."

The Anti-Americans' Position:

In The Communist Manifesto, Karl Marx said:

141. "Abolition of the family! Even the most radical flare up at this infamous proposal of the Communists."

142. "The bourgeois family will vanish as a matter of course when its complement vanishes, and both will vanish with the vanishing of capital."

Abolishing Freedom of Speech

The First Amendment to the Constitution guarantees our right to freedom of speech. It says:

143. "Congress shall make no law respecting an establishment of religion, or prohibiting the free exercise thereof; or abridging the freedom of speech, or of the press; or the right of the people peaceably to assemble, and to petition the Government for a redress of grievances."

Since the Constitution prohibits government officials from openly suppressing freedom of speech, they've outsourced the job to social media platforms. And getting them to silence those who oppose them.

They are censoring everyone who opposes the Marxist Agenda.

The Patriots' Position:

144. "If the freedom of speech is taken away then dumb and silent we may be led, like sheep to the slaughter."—George Washington

Benjamin Franklin said:

145. "Without freedom of thought, there can be no such thing as wisdom; and no such thing as public liberty without freedom of speech."

146. "This sacred privilege is so essential to free governments, that the security of property, and the freedom of speech always go together; and in those wretched countries where a man cannot call his tongue his own, he can scarce call anything else his own... Whoever would overthrow the liberty of a nation must begin by subduing the freeness of speech."

147. "Freedom of speech is a principal pillar of a free government; when this support is taken away, the Constitution of a free society is dissolved, and tyranny is erected on its ruins."

The Anti-Americans' Position:

148. "The children who know how to think for themselves spoil the harmony of the collective society which is coming, where everyone would be interdependent."—John Dewey

149. "Liberating tolerance, then, would mean intolerance against movements from the Right, and toleration of movements from the Left." – Herbert Marcuse

Abolishing Freedom of Religion

In 17th-century England, the Church of England was the official state religion. The religious and government authorities were the same people. They persecuted everyone who disagreed with them. They imprisoned some of them and put others to death.

The Pilgrims came here to escape from this tyranny, and to worship God according to the dictates of their conscience. The Founding Fathers created a nation where everyone is free to choose their own religion.

The Patriots' Position:

150. "Our Ancestors founded their government on morality and religious sentiment. They were brought hither by their high veneration of the Christian religion. They journeyed by its light, and labored in its hope. They sought to incorporate it with the elements of their society, and to diffuse its influences through all their institutions, civil, political, social, and educational."—Daniel Webster

George Washington said:

151. "The liberty enjoyed by the people of these states of worshiping Almighty God agreeably to their conscience, is not only among the choicest of their blessings, but also of their rights."

152. "I have often expressed my sentiments, that every man, conducting himself as a good citizen, and being accountable to God alone for his religious opinions, ought to be protected in worshipping the Deity according to the dictates of his own conscience."

Ronald Reagan said:

153. "Freedom prospers when religion is vibrant and the rule of law under God is acknowledged. When our Founding Fathers passed the First Amendment, they sought to protect churches from government interference. They never intended to construct a wall of hostility between government and the concept of religious belief itself..."

154. "To those who cite the First Amendment as reason for excluding God from more and more of our institutions every day, I say: The First Amendment of the Constitution was not written to protect the people of this country from religious values; it was written to protect religious values from government tyranny."

The Anti-Americans' Position:

155. "Our propaganda necessarily includes the propaganda of atheism."
—Vladimir Lenin

Destroying the Bible

For more than three hundred years, the Bible was America's primary textbook. Its words shaped our morals, tempered our character, and defined our unique American culture. There was a time when every educated person in America was familiar with the Bible.

Then, in 1963, the U. S. Supreme Court made it illegal to teach the Bible in our public schools. And in 1990, they made it illegal to post a copy of the Ten Commandments in them.

Today, millions of young Americans know nothing about the Bible, and this lack of knowledge is destroying our society.

156. "All the miseries and evils which men suffer from vice, crime, ambition, injustice, oppression, slavery and war, proceed from their despising or neglecting the precepts contained in the Bible."—Noah Webster

The Patriots' Position:

Benjamin Rush said:

157. "The only means of establishing and perpetuating our republican forms of government is the universal education of our youth in the principles of Christianity by means of the Bible."

158. "The Bible, when not read in schools, is seldom read in any subsequent period of life... The Bible should be read in our schools in preference to all other books because it contains the greatest portion of that kind of knowledge which is calculated to produce private and public happiness."

159. "The great enemy of the salvation of man, in my opinion, never invented a more effective means of limiting Christianity from the world than by persuading mankind that it was improper to read the Bible at schools."

Daniel Webster said:

160. "If truth is not diffused, error will be; If God and his word are not known and received, the devil and his works will gain the ascendancy. If the evangelical volume does not reach every hamlet, the pages of a corrupt and licentious literature will. If the power of the Gospel is not felt throughout the length and breadth of the land, anarchy and misrule, degradation and misery, corruption and darkness will reign without mitigation or end."

Destroying Christianity

The Bible says there is a way that seems right unto a man, but its end is the way of death. And communism certainly fits that description. It looks good in theory, but it doesn't work out in practice. And it certainly leads people to their deaths. In the twentieth century, a hundred million people were casualties of communism. And most of them were murdered.

Even though communism has failed every time it has been tried, the communists fully expect Karl Marx's promises to be fulfilled. And for communism to destroy Christianity and take its place.

The Bible says that the wisdom of God is foolishness to man. And the wisdom of man is certainly foolishness to God.

161. "For the preaching of the cross is to them that perish foolishness; but unto us which are saved it is the power of God. For it is written, I will destroy the wisdom of the wise, and will bring to nothing the understanding of the prudent.

"Where is the wise? where is the scribe? where is the disputer of this world? hath not God made foolish the wisdom of this world?

"For after that in the wisdom of God the world by wisdom knew not God, it pleased God by the foolishness of preaching to save them that believe."

162. "But God hath chosen the foolish things of the world to confound the wise; and God hath chosen the weak things of the world to confound the things which are mighty; And base things of the world, and things which are despised, hath God chosen, yea, and things which are not, to bring to nought things that are: That no flesh should glory in his presence."

163. "But when the fullness of time had come, God sent forth his Son, born of woman, born under the law, to redeem those who were under the law, so that we might receive adoption as sons. And because you are sons, God has sent the Spirit of his Son into our hearts, crying, 'Abba! Father!' So you are no longer a slave, but a son, and if a son, then an heir through God."

This is the truth of the Gospel of Jesus Christ. Our enemies want to keep people from hearing it—by any means necessary. Because faith comes by hearing and hearing by the word of God.

The Patriots' Position:

164. "The religion which has introduced civil liberty is the religion of Christ and His apostles, which enjoins humility, piety, and benevolence; which acknowledges in every person a brother, or a sister, and a citizen with equal rights. This is genuine Christianity, and to this we owe our free Constitution of Government."—Noah Webster

165. "While we are zealously performing the duties of good citizens and soldiers, we certainly ought not to be inattentive to the higher duties of religion. To the distinguished character of Patriot, it should be our highest glory to add the more distinguished character of Christian."— George Washington

166. "My views... are the result of a life of inquiry and reflection, and very different from the anti-Christian system imputed to me by those who know nothing of my opinions. To the corruptions of Christianity I am, indeed, opposed; but not to the genuine precepts of Jesus himself. I am a Christian in the only sense in which He wished any one to be: sincerely attached to his doctrines in preference to all others..."— Thomas Jefferson

The Anti-Americans' Position:

Joseph Goebbels said:

167. "What does Christianity mean today? National Socialism is a religion. All we lack is a religious genius capable of uprooting outmoded religious practices and putting new ones in their place.

"We lack traditions and ritual. One day soon, National Socialism will be the religion of all Germans. My party is my church, and I believe I serve the Lord best if I do his will, and liberate my oppressed people from the fetters of slavery. That is my gospel.

"The war we are fighting until victory or the bitter end is in its deepest sense a war between Christ and Marx. Christ: the principle of love. Marx: the principle of hate."

Abolishing Morality

Morality is essential to preserving our God-given freedoms. When Dr. Timothy Dwight became President of Yale College, he fired every professor who followed the teachings of the French Revolution — that morality is possible apart from God and the Bible. He said:

168. "Education ought everywhere to be religious education. Parents are bound to employ instructors who will educate their children religiously. To commit our children to the care of irreligious persons is to commit lambs to the superintendency of wolves."

The Patriots' Position:

Daniel Webster said:

169. "Our ancestors established their system of government on morality and religious sentiment. Moral habits, they believed, cannot safely be trusted on any other foundation than religious principle, nor any government be secure which is not supported by moral habits ... Whatever makes men good Christians, makes them good citizens ..."

170. "To preserve the government we must also preserve morals. Morality rests on religion; if you destroy the foundation, the superstructure must fall. When the public mind becomes vitiated and corrupt, laws are a nullity and constitutions are waste paper."

Samuel Adams said:

171. "It is in the interest of tyrants to reduce the people to ignorance and vice. For they cannot live in any country where virtue and knowledge prevail. The religion and public liberty of a people are intimately connected; their interests are interwoven, they cannot subsist separately; and therefore they rise and fall together. For this reason, it is always observable, that those who are combined to destroy the people's liberties, practice every art to poison their morals."

172. "No people will tamely surrender their Liberties, nor can any be easily subdued, when knowledge is diffused and Virtue is preserved. On the Contrary, when People are universally ignorant, and debauched in their Manners, they will sink under their own weight without the Aid of foreign Invaders."

173. "If virtue & knowledge are diffused among the People, they will never be enslav'd. This will be their great security."

174. "Liberty will not long survive the total extinction of morals."

The Anti-Americans' Position:

175. "We say that our morality is entirely subordinated to the interests of the proletariat's class struggle. Our morality stems from the interests of the class struggle of the proletariat."—Vladimir Lenin

Ronald Reagan explained the Marxists' concept of morality. He said:

176. "During my first press conference as President, in answer to a direct question, I pointed out that, as good Marxist-Leninists, the Soviet leaders have openly and publicly declared that the only morality they recognize is that which will further their cause, which is world revolution.

"I think I should point out I was only quoting Lenin, their guiding spirit, who said in 1920 that they repudiate all morality that proceeds from supernatural ideas — that's their name for religion — or ideas that are outside class conceptions. Morality is entirely subordinate to the interests of class war. And everything is moral that is necessary for the annihilation of the old, exploiting social order and for uniting the proletariat."

Ignoring the Constitution

The United States of America is a constitutional republic. Our Constitution separates the powers of government into three separate and equal branches: The Legislative Branch makes the laws. The Executive Branch enforces the laws, and the Judicial Branch interprets the Laws. This separation of powers of government is essential to the preservation of our liberty.

This is antithetical to the Marxists' vision of a government with unlimited powers. It tells its people what they can and cannot do. And it requires them to sacrifice everything they have for "the common good."

The Patriots' Position:

177. "The greatest danger to American freedom is a government that ignores the Constitution."—Thomas Jefferson

178. "Liberty once lost is lost forever. When the People once surrender their share in the Legislature, and their Right of defending the Limitations upon the Government, and of resisting every Encroachment upon them, they can never regain it."—John Adams

Abraham Lincoln said:

179. "Don't interfere with anything in the Constitution. That must be maintained, for it is the only safeguard of our liberties."

180. "We the people are the rightful masters of both Congress and the courts, not to overthrow the Constitution but to overthrow the men who pervert the Constitution."

Daniel Webster said:

181. "Hold on, my friends, to the Constitution and to the Republic for which it stands. Miracles do not cluster and what has happened once in 6,000 years, may not happen again. Hold on to the Constitution, for if the American Constitution should fail, there will be anarchy throughout the world."

Abolishing the Rule of Law

The Constitution and the Bill of Rights are the law of the land. And they're based on our unalienable rights to life, liberty, and property. Unalienable rights are rights that are given to us by God. The government didn't give them to us, and the government can't take them away.

The Bill of Rights tells the government what it cannot do. It cannot deny our rights to freedom of speech, freedom of religion, freedom of the press, the right to assemble peaceably and to petition the government for a redress of our grievances. And it cannot infringe upon our right to keep and bear arms.

The Patriots' Position:

James Madison said:

182. *"The essence of Government is power; and power, lodged as it must be in human hands, will ever be liable to abuse."*

183. *"All men having power ought to be distrusted to a certain degree."*

184. *"The accumulation of all powers, legislative, executive, and judiciary, in the same hands, whether of one, a few, or many, and whether hereditary, self-appointed, or elective, may justly be pronounced the very definition of tyranny."*

Alexander Hamilton said:

185. *"The instrument by which it [government] must act are either the AUTHORITY of the laws or FORCE. If the first be destroyed, the last must be substituted; and where this becomes the ordinary instrument of government there is an end to liberty!"*

The Anti-Americans' Position:

Vladimir Lenin said,

186. *"Dictatorship is rule based directly upon force and unrestricted by any laws. The revolutionary dictatorship of the proletariat is rule won and maintained by the use of violence by the proletariat against the bourgeoisie, rule that is unrestricted by any laws."*

187. *"Soviet power is a new type of state in which there is no bureaucracy, no police, no standing army."*

188. *"The very essence of the struggle for power is the use of force. The State is founded on power; it must be maintained by power."* – A. Hitler

Confiscating All Guns and Ammunition

Communist China has the largest standing army in the world with two million members. However, the United States has over one hundred-million-gun owners. There are nineteen million veterans who are well-trained in the use of firearms. As are the five million members of the

National Rifle Association. We are what James Madison called a well-regulated militia. He said:

189. "A well regulated militia, composed of the body of the people, trained to arms is the best and most natural defense of a free country."

James Madison was the principal author of the Bill of Rights, including the Second Amendment, which says:

190. "A well regulated Militia, being necessary to the security of a free State, the right of the people to keep and bear Arms, shall not be infringed."

The Second Amendment doesn't grant us the right to keep and bear arms. It prohibits the government from infringing on our right to do so. Our arms are for self-defense, and they're also an insurance policy to protect us from government tyranny.

The American Marxists want to shame us into disarming ourselves. And if that doesn't work, they plan on disarming us. When they talk about gun control, they mean gun confiscation. Every bit of legislation they propose is another step toward that goal. And it's always under the guise of keeping us safe.

The Patriots' Position:

191. "Among the natural rights of the Colonists are these: First, a right to life; Secondly, to liberty; Thirdly, to property; together with the right to support and defend them in the best manner they can. These are evident branches of, rather than deductions from, the duty of self-preservation, commonly called the first law of nature."—Samuel Adams

192. "To disarm the people... is the most effectual way to enslave them."—George Mason

193. "Before a standing army can rule, the people must be disarmed, as they are in almost every country in Europe. The supreme power in

America cannot enforce unjust laws by the sword; because the whole body of the people are armed, and constitute a force superior to any band of regular troops."—Noah Webster

The Anti-Americans' Position:

194. "Every Communist must grasp the truth 'Political power grows out of the barrel of a gun.' Our principle is that the Communist Party commands the gun and the gun will never be allowed to command the Party."—Mao Zedong

195. "If the opposition disarms, well and good. If it refuses to disarm, we shall disarm it ourselves."—Joseph Stalin

Confiscating All Our Assets

The Federal government is confiscating our money in two different ways. They're stealing our income through excessive taxation and stealing our wealth through inflation. And they would love to eliminate all rights of inheritance.

John Maynard Keynes was a British economist, and he was also a Fabian Socialist. Our government's fiscal policies are based on Keynesian Economics and deficit spending. Deficit spending is spending money we don't have. And it is the chief cause of inflation. At present, our national debt is $37 trillion, and it's increasing rapidly.

This is what Keynes said about inflation:

196. "By a continuing process of inflation, governments can confiscate, secretly and unobserved, an important part of the wealth of their citizens."

197. "Inflation is not caused by the actions of private citizens, but by the government."—Ayn Rand

198. *"The advocates of public control cannot do without inflation. They need it in order to finance their policy of reckless spending and of lavishly subsidizing and bribing the voters."*—Ludwig von Mises

The Patriots' Position

199. *"The collection of taxes which are not absolutely required, which do not beyond reasonable doubt contribute to the public welfare is only a species of legalized larceny."*—Calvin Coolidge

Thomas Jefferson said:

200. *"I am not among those who fear the people. They and not the rich, are our dependence for continued freedom. And to preserve their independence, we must not let our rulers load us with perpetual debt..."*

201. *"I sincerely believe that banking establishments are more dangerous than standing armies, and that the principle of spending money to be paid by posterity under the name of funding is but swindling futurity on a large scale."*

The Anti-Americans' Position

202. *"Hundreds of thousands of rouble notes are being issued daily by our treasury. This is done, not in order to fill the coffers of the State with practically worthless paper, but with the deliberate intention of destroying the value of money as a means of payment... Experience has taught us it is impossible to root out the evils of capitalism merely by confiscation and expropriation...*

"The simplest way to exterminate the very spirit of capitalism is therefore to flood the country with notes of a high face-value without financial guarantees of any sort... Men will cease to covet and hoard it so soon as they discover it will not buy anything, and the great illusion of the value and power of money, on which the capitalist state is based will have been definitely destroyed."—Vladimir Lenin

Destroying the American Middle Class

The American Marxists are using the Nazis' propaganda techniques to recruit people to be part of the Communist Revolution. Joseph Goebbels said:

203. "There are two ways to make a revolution. You can blast your enemy with machine guns until he acknowledges the superiority of those holding the machine guns. That is one way. Or you can transform the nation through a revolution of the spirit..."

The American Marxists developed a cult of personality surrounding Barack Obama. He campaigned on a platform of "Hope and Change." But he failed to mention that the "Change" would be from capitalism to socialism.

In a campaign speech in Columbia, Missouri, on October 30, 2008, Barack Obama said:

204. "We are five days away from fundamentally transforming the United States of America."

Michelle Obama gave us a preview of what was in store for us when she said,

205. "Barack knows that we are going to have to make sacrifices; we are going to have to change our conversation; we're going to have to change our traditions, our history; we're going to have to move into a different place as a nation."

That's because, as Karl Marx said in *The Communist Manifesto*:

206. "For us the issue cannot be the alteration of private property but only its annihilation, not the smoothing over of class antagonisms but the abolition of classes not the improvement of the existing society but the foundation of a new one."

This was Vladimir Lenin's definition of the term "democracy":

207. "A democracy is a state which recognizes the subjection of the minority to the majority, that is, an organization for the systematic use of violence by one class against the other, by one part of the population against another."

Karl Marx explained that in the Revolution, the money and property of the middle class (the bourgeoisie) will be confiscated and redistributed to the working class (the proletariat). He said:

208. "We have seen above, that the first step in the revolution by the working class is to raise the proletariat to the position of ruling class to win the battle of democracy."

"The proletariat will use its political supremacy to wrest by degree, all capital from the bourgeoisie, to centralise all instruments of production in the hands of the State, i.e., of the proletariat organised as the ruling class; and to increase the total productive forces as rapidly as possible.

The Biden-Harris Administration allowed twenty-one million illegal immigrants to enter our country. And gave them free money, food, hotel rooms, air travel, health care, college tuition, and cell phones.

American taxpayers paid billions of dollars for these things. And the future cost of this giant give-away program is incalculable. Because our children and grandchildren will be paying higher taxes to the federal government, and their state and local governments forever.

This massive redistribution of wealth is the hallmark of communism, and it is most certainly unconstitutional. James Madison was the Father of the Constitution, and he said:

209. "The government of the United States is a definite government, confined to specified objects. It is not like the state governments, whose powers are more general. Charity is no part of the legislative duty of the government."

The Federal government was intended to be a limited government. The Preamble of the Constitution defines what it's supposed to be doing. It says:

210. "We the People of the United States, in Order to form a more perfect Union, establish Justice, insure domestic Tranquility, provide for the common defence, promote the general Welfare, and secure the Blessings of Liberty to ourselves and our Posterity, do ordain and establish this Constitution for the United States of America."

The Patriots' Position:

James Madison was the principal author of the United States Constitution.

211. Madison said he could not undertake to lay his finger on that article of the Constitution which granted a right of Congress of expending, on objects of benevolence, the money of their constituents.

The redistribution of wealth by the government is, and has always been, unconstitutional.

212. "The utopian schemes of leveling and a community of goods, are as visionary and impractical as those which vest all property in the crown. These ideas are arbitrary, despotic, and in our government, unconstitutional." -- Samuel Adams

In 1850, French economist Frédéric Bastiat published *The Law*. It was a rebuttal to *The Communist Manifesto*.

Bastiat explained that socialism is merely legalized plunder. He said:

213. "When plunder becomes a way of life for a group of men in a society, over the course of time they create for themselves a legal system that authorizes it and a moral code that glorifies it."

214. "But how is this legal plunder to be identified? Quite simply. See if the law takes from some persons what belongs to them and gives it to

other persons to whom it does not belong. See if the law benefits one citizen at the expense of another by doing what the citizen himself cannot do without committing a crime."

The American Marxists' Big Lie

Adolph Hitler said to imprint the Big Lie on the public mind, they must confine propaganda to a few simple ideas, and they must repeat them constantly. The present Big Lie of the American Marxists is that America is such an incredibly racist nation that it is beyond repair. It must be destroyed and transformed into a socialist state because socialism is fair, and capitalism is not.

They insist that capitalism, individualism, and meritocracy are based on racism. And they must be replaced by diversity, equity, and inclusion (DEI).

The False Gospel of Wokeism

There's a new religion being taught in America today, and it's based on the following false assumptions:

- All white people are racists simply because they are white.
- It's impossible for black people to be racists because they don't have the power to oppress other racial groups.
- All white people must confess their sin of racism, repent of it, and make a public profession of faith in these precepts. This is called "Going Woke."
- Everyone in America must bow their knee to this new religion of Wokeism.

In the Sermon on the Mount, Jesus warned us to:

215. "Beware of false prophets, which come to you in sheep's clothing, but inwardly they are ravening wolves."

The Apostle Paul warned the Galatian Christians against believing in a false gospel. He said:

216. "I marvel that ye are so soon removed from him that called you into the grace of Christ unto another gospel: Which is not another; but there be some that trouble you, and would pervert the gospel of Christ.

"But though we, or an angel from heaven, preach any other gospel unto you than that which we have preached unto you, let him be accursed. ... For do I now persuade men, or God? or do I seek to please men? for if I yet pleased men, I should not be the servant of Christ.

"But I certify you, brethren, that the gospel which was preached of me is not after man. For I neither received it of man, neither was I taught it, but by the revelation of Jesus Christ."

The Goal of Socialism is Communism

For the communists, socialism is merely a temporary transition between capitalism and communism. There are two requirements for a true communist society to exist. The Communist Party must control all the world's assets, natural resources, and means of production, including the land. And it must also enslave every person on earth.

This was Karl Marx's description of the truly communist society:

217. "In a higher phase of communist society, after the enslaving subordination of the individual to the division of labor, and therewith also the antithesis between mental and physical labor has vanished; after the productive forces have also increased with the all-around development of the individual, after labor has become not only a means of life but life's prime want; and all the springs of co-operative wealth flow more abundantly—only then can the narrow horizon of bourgeois right be crossed in its entirety and society inscribe on its banners: From each according to his ability, to each according to his needs!"

Joseph Stalin explained the steps for creating this utopian society:

218. "Until the bourgeoisie is completely vanquished, until its wealth has been confiscated, the proletariat must without fail possess a military force, it must without fail have its 'proletarian guard,' with the aid of which it will repel the counter-revolutionary attacks of the dying bourgeoisie, exactly as the proletariat did during the Commune."

The communists point to the Paris Commune of 1871 as an example of the "dictatorship of the proletariat." Most Americans have never heard of the Paris Commune. It was mob rule, the same kind of government the Marxists want to impose on the United States of America.

Winston Churchill said:

219. "Those who fail to learn from history are doomed to repeat it."

According to Marx and Lenin, the dictatorship of the proletariat will be essential at first. But after a while, no government will be necessary. Because communist society will be perfect, a kind of heaven on earth.

In this "Workers' Paradise," there will be no crime because there will be no poverty. Because everyone will receive what they need. (And that would be determined by a central planning committee, of course.)

In a true communist society, there will be no incentives to work and earn a reward. And everyone will receive barely enough to sustain life, except for the ruling class elites.

This is Joseph Stalin's description of a true communist society:

220. "Only when we succeed in creating such an order under which people receive for their labor from the society not according to the quantity and quality of labor, but according to their needs will it be possible to say that we have built up a communist society."

The Marxists are conditioning us to believe "you will own nothing, and you will be happy." But that will never happen because communism is slavery. And people will never be happy being slaves to a communist state.

Karl Marx said:

221. "The existence of the state is inseparable from the existence of slavery."

Vladimir Lenin said:

222. "As long as the state exists, there is no freedom. Where there is freedom, there will be no state."

Nobody is going to willingly choose slavery over freedom. That's why Marxism is based on trickery and deception, and everything the Marxists say is a lie. They believe:

- If they make the lie big and tell it often, people will believe it.
- A lie told often enough becomes the truth.

Part Three: The Hope We Have

Did you ever wonder how the American colonists, who had no army or navy, defeated the most powerful military force in the world?

I've found some quotes from the Founding Fathers that explain how they did it. It's a breadcrumb trail of clues that serve as a blueprint for us to follow. And if we follow their example, we will defeat our enemies too.

The Founding Fathers believed in God, and they trusted in him to help them. They were in one accord. And when they said, "Give me liberty or give me death," they meant it. Because they would rather die on their feet than live on their knees.

Samuel Adams described the hope they had. He said:

223. "We have proclaimed to the world our determination 'to die freemen, rather than to live slaves.' We have appealed to Heaven for the justice of our cause, and in Heaven we have placed our trust. Numerous have been the manifestations of God's Providence in sustaining us.

"We have been reduced to distress, and the arm of Omnipotence has raised us up. Let us still rely in humble confidence on Him who is mighty to save. Good tidings will soon arrive. We shall never be abandoned by Heaven while we act worthy of its aid and protection."

These were George Washington's inspiring words to his army at the beginning of the Revolutionary War:

224. "The time is now near at hand which must probably determine whether Americans are to be freemen or slaves; whether they are to have any property they can call their own; whether their houses and farms are to be pillaged and destroyed, and themselves consigned to a state of wretchedness from which no human effort will deliver them."

"The fate of unborn millions will now depend, under God, on the courage and conduct of this army. Our cruel and unrelenting enemy leaves us only the choice of brave resistance, or the most abject submission. We have therefore to resolve to conquer or die."

Benjamin Franklin believed in God, and he believed in the power of prayer. When he was a delegate to the Constitutional Convention at Independence Hall in Philadelphia in 1789, he was eighty-one years old. At first, they were making no progress. Then, Franklin made a motion to open each day's session with prayer. He said:

225. *"In the beginning of the contest with G. Britain, when we were sensible of danger we had daily prayer in this room for the Divine Protection. — Our prayers, Sir, were heard, and they were graciously answered.*

"All of us who were engaged in the struggle must have observed frequent instances of a Superintending providence in our favor. To that kind providence we owe this happy opportunity of consulting in peace on the means of establishing our future national felicity. And have we now forgotten that powerful friend? Or do we imagine that we no longer need His assistance?"

James Madison said,

226. *"It is impossible for the man of pious reflection not to perceive in it the finger of that Almighty Hand which has been so frequently and signally extended to our relief in the critical stages of the Revolution."*

In his "Give Me Liberty or Give Me Death" speech, Patrick Henry revealed the secret of their success. It was their strong faith in God. He said:

227. *"Sir, we are not weak, if we make a proper use of those forces which the God of nature hath placed in our power. Three millions of people, armed in the holy cause of liberty, and in such a country as that which we possess, are invincible by any force which our enemy can send against us.*

"Besides, sir, we shall not fight this battle alone... There is a just God who presides over the destinies of nations... The battle, sir, is not to the strong alone; it is to the vigilant, the active, the brave...

"What is it that gentlemen wish? What would they have? Is life so dear, or peace so sweet, as to be purchased at the price of chains and slavery? Forbid it, Almighty God! I know not what course others may take; but as for me, give me liberty or give me death!"

In his later writings, Patrick Henry explained why they were invincible against any force the enemy sent against them. It was because of the armor of God. Patrick Henry also explained what the armor of God is, when he said:

228. *"Virtue, morality, and religion. That is the armor my friend. And this alone renders us invincible. These are the tactics that we should study. If we lose these, we are conquered, fallen indeed... so long as our manners and principles remain sound, there is no danger."*

I believe he was referring to the armor of God described in the Bible. In the following passage of Scripture, each element of God's armor corresponds to a part of the Roman soldier's battle gear: The sandals and the helmet. The breastplate and the belt. The sword and the shield. The Bible says:

229. *"Be ready! Let the truth be like a belt around your waist, and let God's justice protect you like armor. Your desire to tell the good news about peace should be like shoes on your feet. Let your faith be like a shield, and you will be able to stop all the flaming arrows of the evil one.*

Let God's saving power be like a helmet, and for a sword use God's message that comes from the Spirit."

The Weapons of our Warfare

If we go on offense against the American Marxists, by taking the following actions, we will defeat them and prevent them from achieving their goals. These are the weapons of our warfare:

- Knowing the Truth
- Speaking the Truth
- Having Faith in God
- Doing What's Right
- Praying Every Day
- Using Our God-Given Gifts
- Informing As Many People as Possible

Knowing the Truth

Freedom is an idea that originated in the mind of God, and he revealed it to us in the Bible. The greatest threat to America today isn't climate change, or systemic racism. It's losing our freedom and being slaves to a socialist state.

Communism is an idea that originated in the mind of Karl Marx. It is a modern-day version of slavery. It's being shoved down our throats every day, in our schools, on television, and on social media. And we're being conditioned to accept it as being inevitable.

But Horace Greeley was certainly right when he said,

230. "It is impossible to enslave, mentally or socially, a bible-reading people. The principles of the Bible are the groundwork of human freedom."

The Bible was America's textbook for over three hundred years. Then, in 1963, the U. S. Supreme Court banned it in our public schools. Now, the Bible is the missing ingredient in our society. And our lack of knowledge of it is destroying us.

Noah Webster said,

231. "All the miseries and evils which men suffer from vice, crime, ambition, injustice, oppression, slavery and war, proceed from their despising or neglecting the precepts contained in the Bible."

Most of what we call common sense was derived from the Bible and passed down through generations of God-fearing parents.

232. Jesus said, "If ye continue in my word, then are ye my disciples indeed; And ye shall know the truth, and the truth shall make you free."

Knowing the truth is an essential requirement for being free. When we know the truth, we can tell when someone is lying to us. We know that America began with people who escaped persecution by a tyrannical government because of their religious beliefs. And we know the United States of America began in 1776.

So, when somebody tells us the United States of America began in 1619, when seven African slaves arrived in Jamestown. And the purpose of the Revolutionary War was to preserve the institution of slavery—we know those are lies. But our children don't know it. All they know is what they're being taught in school.

Somebody must tell them the truth about our nation's history. The First Great Awakening ignited the American Revolution. And the Second

Great Awakening led to the abolition of slavery when President Abraham Lincoln signed the Emancipation Proclamation in 1863.

Every schoolchild in America needs to know these things. And it's up to us, their parents and grandparents, to teach them. Because nobody else is going to do it.

233. "The secret of freedom lies in educating people, whereas the secret of tyranny is in keeping them ignorant."—Maximilien Robespierre

Speaking the Truth

Our enemies, the American Marxists, have no defense against the truth. It's like Kryptonite to them. They know it can destroy them, and they avoid it at all costs. Their most powerful weapon is lying, and ours is speaking the truth.

When we confront them with the truth, they respond with slanderous ad hominem attacks. Because the facts are against them.

John Adams said:

234. "Facts are stubborn things; and whatever may be our wishes, our inclination, or the dictates of our passions, they cannot alter the state of facts and evidence."

George Washington said:

235. "Truth will ultimately prevail where there is pains to bring it to light."

Vladimir Lenin said:

236. "We must be ready to employ trickery, deceit, law-breaking, withholding and concealing truth. ... We can and must write in a

language which sows among the masses hate, revulsion, and scorn toward those who disagree with us."

Having Faith in God

Faith in God has always been the prevailing mindset of the American people. It is, and has always been, the secret of our success. And it's one of the most powerful weapons on earth. Faith in God is the catalyst that causes God to intervene on our behalf.

The Bible says,

237. "But without faith it is impossible to please him: for he that cometh to God must believe that he is, and that he is a rewarder of them that diligently seek him."

238. "The Lord is constantly watching everyone, and he gives strength to those who faithfully obey him."

239. "Oh that my people had hearkened unto me, and Israel had walked in my ways. I should soon have subdued their enemies, and turned my hand against their adversaries."

240. "The men from the tribes of Manasseh, Reuben, and Gad prayed to God during the war, asking him to help them. So, he helped them because they trusted him."

The following quote is from Abraham Lincoln's farewell speech to the citizens of Springfield, Illinois, when he left to become President of the United States. I like to paraphrase it like this: Without God, I cannot succeed. With him, I cannot fail. Abraham Lincoln said:

241. "Without the assistance of that divine being, I cannot succeed. With that assistance I cannot fail. Trusting in Him, who can go with me, remain with you and be everywhere for good let us confidently hope that all will yet be well."

Doing What's Right

In our American culture, we generally follow the Golden Rule. That means loving your neighbor as yourself. When you love your neighbors, you don't lie to them, and you don't steal from them. This is our way of keeping God's commandments or doing what's right.

The Bible says:

242. "And it shall be our righteousness, if we observe to do all these commandments before the Lord our God as he hath commanded us."

243. "The Lord rewarded me because I did what was right, because I did what the Lord said was right."

244. "By our purity, knowledge, and kindness we have shown ourselves to be God's servants by the Holy Spirit, by our true love, by our message of truth and the power of God, we have righteousness as our weapon, both to attack and to defend ourselves."

Samuel Adams said:

245. "In the supposed state of nature, all men are equally bound by the laws of nature, or to speak more properly, the laws of the Creator. They are imprinted by the finger of God on the heart of man. Thou shalt do no injury to thy neighbor, is the voice of nature and reason, and it is confirmed by written revelation."

Praying Every Day

On June 6, 1944, during the Invasion of Normandy, President Franklin D. Roosevelt gave a national radio address. He led the nation in prayer, asking God to help our troops defeat the Nazis. He asked the American people to continue to pray for them every day. They did, and God answered those prayers. This was President Roosevelt's prayer:

246. "Almighty God: Our sons, pride of our Nation, this day have set upon a mighty endeavor, a struggle to preserve our Republic, our religion, and our civilization, and to set free a suffering humanity.

Lead them straight and true; give strength to their arms, stoutness to their hearts, steadfastness in their faith.

They will need Thy blessings. Their road will be long and hard. For the enemy is strong. He may hurl back our forces. Success may not come with rushing speed, but we shall return again and again; and we know that by Thy grace, and by the righteousness of our cause, our sons will triumph.

They will be sore tried, by night and by day, without rest-until the victory is won. The darkness will be rent by noise and flame. Men's souls will be shaken with the violences of war.

For these men are lately drawn from the ways of peace. They fight not for the lust of conquest. They fight to end conquest. They fight to liberate. They fight to let justice arise, and tolerance and good will among all Thy people. They yearn but for the end of battle, for their return to the haven of home.

Some will never return. Embrace these, Father, and receive them, Thy heroic servants, into Thy kingdom.

And for us at home - fathers, mothers, children, wives, sisters, and brothers of brave men overseas - whose thoughts and prayers are ever with them - help us, Almighty God, to rededicate ourselves in renewed faith in Thee in this hour of great sacrifice.

Many people have urged that I call the Nation into a single day of special prayer. But because the road is long and the desire is great, I ask that our people devote themselves in a continuance of prayer. As we rise to each new day, and again when each day is spent, let words of prayer be on our lips, invoking Thy help to our efforts.

Give us strength, too - strength in our daily tasks, to redouble the contributions we make in the physical and the material support of our armed forces.

And let our hearts be stout, to wait out the long travail, to bear sorrows that may come, to impart our courage unto our sons wheresoever they may be.

And, O Lord, give us Faith. Give us Faith in Thee; Faith in our sons; Faith in each other; Faith in our united crusade. Let not the keenness of our spirit ever be dulled. Let not the impacts of temporary events, of temporal matters of but fleeting moment let not these deter us in our unconquerable purpose.

With Thy blessing, we shall prevail over the unholy forces of our enemy. Help us to conquer the apostles of greed and racial arrogancies. Lead us to the saving of our country, and with our sister Nations into a world unity that will spell a sure peace a peace invulnerable to the schemings of unworthy men. And a peace that will let all of men live in freedom, reaping the just rewards of their honest toil.

Thy will be done, Almighty God. Amen."

Our prayers are like heavy artillery in this war against our enemies. Mary, Queen of Scots, is reported to have said she feared John Knox's prayers more than all the assembled armies of Europe. That's because, according to the Bible,

247. "The effectual fervent prayer of a righteous man availeth much."

However, we can't just sit back, do nothing, and expect God to do everything. We have to work like everything depends on us and pray like everything depends on God.

The Bible tells us,

248. "Be careful for nothing; but in every thing by prayer and supplication with thanksgiving let your requests be made known unto God. And the peace of God, which passeth all understanding, shall keep your hearts and minds through Christ Jesus."

249. "If you obey the Lord, he will watch over you and answer your prayers. But God despises evil people, and he will wipe them all from the earth, till they are forgotten. When his people pray for help, he listens and rescues them from their troubles. The Lord is there to rescue all who are discouraged and given up hope."

250. "If my people, which are called by my name, shall humble themselves, and pray, and seek my face, and turn from their wicked ways; then will I hear from heaven, and will forgive their sin, and will heal their land."

Using Our God Given Gifts

God wants us to use the gifts he gave us. And to take what we've learned and pass it on to others, especially to our own children.

251. "And Christ gave gifts to people—he made some to be apostles, some to be prophets, some to go and tell the Good News, and some to have the work of caring for and teaching God's people. Christ gave those gifts to prepare God's holy people for the work of serving, to make the body of Christ stronger. This work must continue until we are all joined together in the same faith and in the same knowledge of the Son of God. We must become like a mature person, growing until we become like Christ and have his perfection."

252. "Then we will no longer be babies. We will not be tossed about like a ship that the waves carry one way and then another. We will not be influenced by every new teaching we hear from people who are trying to fool us. They make plans and try any kind of trick to fool people into following the wrong path. No! Speaking the truth with love, we will grow up in every way into Christ, who is the head. The whole body depends on Christ, and all the parts of the body are joined and held together. Each part does its own work to make the whole body grow and be strong with love."

Informing as Many People as Possible

"Give light, and the people will find their own way." That's the motto of the Scripts-Howard newspaper chain, and it's also the purpose of this book.

The Marxists don't want people to know the truth about America's founding or the truth about socialism and communism. When people know the truth about these things, the Marxist propagandists can't deceive them anymore.

Conclusion

We are the American Patriot Community. We are the spiritual descendants of the people who founded America, and the people who fought and died to preserve it. We are people of all races, all ethnicities, all social and economic backgrounds. And we are united by our faith in God.

Ronald Reagan explained the challenge that lies before us. He said:

253. *"Freedom is never more than one generation away from extinction. We didn't pass it to our children in the bloodstream. It must be fought for, protected, and handed on for them to do the same, or one day we will spend our sunset years telling our children and our children's children what it was once like in the United States where men were free."*

254. *"You and I have a rendezvous with destiny. We will preserve for our children this, the last best hope of man on earth, or we will sentence them to take the first step into a thousand years of darkness. If we fail, at least let our children and our children's children say of us we justified our brief moment here. We did all that could be done."*

255. *"The struggle now going on for the world will never be decided by bombs or rockets, by armies or military might. The real crisis we face today is a spiritual one; at root, it is a test of moral will and faith."*

256. *"Above all, we must realize that no arsenal, or no weapon in the arsenal of the world, is so formidable as the will and moral courage of free men and women. It is a weapon our adversaries in today's world do not have."*

We must push back against our domestic enemies, the American Marxists, and defeat them all at the ballot box. They are the greatest threat to our liberty and freedom. We must be the army that Thomas Jefferson referred to in his writings. He said:

257. "The functionaries of every government have propensities to command at will the liberty and property of their constituents. There is no safe deposit for these but with the people themselves; nor can they be safe with them without information. Where the press is free, and every man able to read, all is safe."

258. "A sense of this necessity, and a submission to it, is to me a new and consolatory proof that wherever the people are well informed they can be trusted with their own government; that whenever things get so far wrong as to attract their notice, they may be relied on to set them to rights."

259. "The good sense of the people will always be found the best army. They may be led astray for a moment, but will soon correct themselves."

We are American patriots like George Washington, John Adams, Benjamin Franklin, and Thomas Jefferson. They weren't perfect and neither are we. But God loves us anyway, and he will fight for us just as he did for them. That is the hope we have.

This is Our Mission

We are an army of volunteers. We are happy warriors, and these are our standing orders. When we're doing these things, we're putting on the whole armor of God. We're walking by faith. We're doing what's right. And we're trusting in God to help us.

260. *"In the Lord's name, I tell you this. Do not continue living like those who do not believe. Their thoughts are worth nothing. They do not understand, and they know nothing, because they refuse to listen. So they cannot have the life that God gives. They have lost all feeling of shame, and they use their lives for doing evil. They continually want to do all kinds of evil."*

261. *"But what you learned in Christ was not like this. I know that you heard about him, and you are in him, so you were taught the truth that is in Jesus. You were taught to leave your old self—to stop living the evil way you lived before. That old self becomes worse, because people are fooled by the evil things they want to do. But you were taught to be made new in your hearts, to become a new person. That new person is made to be like God—made to be truly good and holy."*

262. *"So you must stop telling lies. Tell each other the truth, because we all belong to each other in the same body. When you are angry, do not sin, and be sure to stop being angry before the end of the day. Do not give the devil a way to defeat you. Those who are stealing must stop stealing and start working. They should earn an honest living for themselves. Then they will have something to share with those who are poor."*

263. *"When you talk, do not say harmful things, but say what people need—words that will help others become stronger. Then what you say will do good to those who listen to you. And do not make the Holy Spirit sad. The Spirit is God's proof that you belong to him. God gave you the Spirit to show that God will make you free when the final day comes. Do not be bitter or angry or mad. Never shout angrily or say things to hurt others. Never do anything evil. Be kind and loving to each other, and forgive each other just as God forgave you in Christ."*

There are tens of millions of us American patriots. And we are invincible against any force the enemy can send against us. Because there is a just God who presides over the destinies of nations. He will fight for us and give us victory over all our enemies.

Before You Go

I truly hope *The Good, The Bad, & The Hope We Have: A Treasury of Useful Quotations* has encouraged you, made you think, or lifted your spirit in some way.

If it did, I'd be so grateful if you'd take a quick moment to leave a short review on Amazon. Your feedback really helps others to decide if this book might be right for them.

Thank you so much for reading, and for being part of this journey of faith, freedom, and hope.

With gratitude,

Larry Vaughn

About the Author

Larry Vaughn is an inspirational nonfiction author whose writing calls readers to stand firm in faith, cherish freedom, and remember the timeless principles that shaped America. Through his three Christian books, Larry weaves history, biblical truth, and patriotic conviction into a powerful message for today's generation.

Larry and his wife, Marie, have been married for fifty-eight years and enjoy life on their farm in Tennessee. You can follow them on these websites:

www.biblebelieverspublishing.com

www.facebook.com/LarryandMarie

www.instagram.com/bible.believers.publishing

www.larryvaughnbooks.com

www.pinterest.com/BibleBelieversPublishing

www.tiktok.com/@biblebelieverspublishing

www.x.com/@TheBibleGuy

www.youtube.com/@LarryandMarie

Notes

1. William F. Buckley, Jr., *God and Man at Yale*, (Washington DC: Regnery Publishing, 1951).

2. Abraham Lincoln, "House Divided Speech," Springfield, Illinois (June 16, 1858).

3. Luke 6:45, King James Version.

4. Karl Marx, *The Communist Manifesto*, Ch. 2.

5. Vladimir Lenin, as quoted in *The Proletarian Revolution and the Renegade Kautsky* (1972), p. 11.

6. John Dewey, "Soul-Searching," Teacher Magazine, September 1933, p. 33.

7. Noah Webster, Preface to the 1828 edition of *Webster's American Dictionary of the English Language*, 1828.

8. John Adams, "From John Adams to Hezekiah Niles, 13 February 1818."

9. Karl Marx, *The Communist Manifesto*, Chap. 4.

10. Ronald Reagan, Farewell Address to the Nation, January 11, 1989.

11. "From Thomas Jefferson to Edward Carrington, 16 January 1787."

12. The Declaration of Independence.

13. Deuteronomy 20:4, ESV.

14. Benjamin Rush: To Elias Boudinot on July 9, 1788. *Letters of Benjamin Rush*, L. H. Butterfield, ed., (American Philosophical Society, 1951), Vol. 1, p. 475.

15. Benjamin Rush: Address to the People of the United States, American Museum, January 1787.

16. Julia Ward Howe, "Battle Hymn of the Republic," 1861.

17. U. S. Const. amend. XIII.

18. U. S. Const. amend. XIV.

19. U. S. Const. amend. XV.

20. John Adams, A Dissertation on the Canon and Feudal Law, The Works of John Adams, Volume 10, p. 1850 – 1856.

21. John Adams, The Works of John Adams, Second President of the United States, Charles Francis Adams, editor (Boston: Charles C. Little and James Brown, 1851), Vol. VI, p. 9.)

22. "John Adams to Thomas Jefferson, 28 June 1813," *The Papers of Thomas Jefferson*, Retirement Series, vol. 6, *11 March to 27 November 1813*, ed. J. Jefferson Looney. Princeton: Princeton University Press, 2009, pp. 236–239.

23. "John Adams to Abigail Adams, 7 July 1775," Original source: *The Adams Papers*, Adams Family Correspondence, vol. 1, *December 1761 – May 1776*, ed. Lyman H. Butterfield. Cambridge, MA: Harvard University Press, 1963, pp. 241–243.

24. Samuel Adams (1906). "The Writings of Samuel Adams: 1770-1773".

25. Samuel Adams, "The Rights of the Colonists", November 20, 1772.

26. Ibid.

27. Samuel Adams, letter to James Warren, October 24, 1780.

28. Samuel Adams, Speech at the Philadelphia State House, August 1, 1776.

29. Benjamin Franklin, "Christian Life and Character of the Civil Institutions of the United States" (Ed. 1864).

30. Benjamin Franklin, "Articles of Belief and Acts of Religion" (20 Nov. 1728).

31. Benjamin Franklin, "Examination before the Committee of the Whole of the House of Commons, 13 February 1766."

32. Ibid.

33. Thomas Jefferson, "Summary View of the Rights of British America" (1774).

34. Thomas Jefferson to Philadelphia Citizens, 1809.

35. Thomas Jefferson, letter to Thomas Cooper, November 29, 1802.

36. Thomas Jefferson, "A Bill for Establishing Religious Freedom."

37. George Washington, "General Orders, 2 July 1776."

38. George Washington, "General Orders, 23 August 1776."

39. George Washington's First Inaugural Address, April 30, 1789.

40. James Madison, "Property," March 29, 1792 issue of the "National Gazette."

41. Ibid.

42. Ibid.

43. Alexander Hamilton, *The Farmer Refuted*, February 1775.

44. Alexander Hamilton, "New York Ratifying Convention. Remarks (Francis Childs' Version), (27 June 1788).

45. Alexander Hamilton, "Tully No. III, (28 August 1794)."

46. "Constitutional Convention. Remarks on the Term of Office for Members of the Second Branch of the Legislature, (26 June 1787)."

47. Noah Webster, *Value of the Bible and Excellence of the Christian Religion For the Use of Families and Schools* (New Haven, CT, 1834), p. 177.

48. Noah Webster, *History of the United States* (New Haven: Durrie and Peck, 1832) pp. 336-337.

49. Abraham Lincoln, The Gettysburg Address, November 19, 1863.

50. President John F. Kennedy's Inaugural Address, January 20, 1961.

51. Ibid.

52. Ibid.

53. Ronald Reagan, Remarks to the Annual Convention of the Concerned Women of America, September 25, 1987.

54. Ronald Reagan, Remarks at the National Conference of the Building and Construction Trades Department, AFL-CIO, March 30, 1981.

55. Ronald Reagan, Farewell Address to the Nation, January 11, 1989.

56. Ronald Reagan, A Time for Choosing Speech, October 27, 1964.

57. Samuel Adams, "The Rights of the Colonists," (November 20, 1772).

58. John F. Kennedy's Message to Chairman Khrushchev Concerning the Meaning of Events in Cuba (18 April 1961).

59. President John F. Kennedy's Inaugural Address (1961).

60. Ibid.

61. Abraham Lincoln, The Gettysburg Address (November 19, 1863).

62. Ludwig von Mises, *Marxism Unmasked: From Delusion to Destruction*, Foundation for Economic Education (2006).

63. The Bay State Monthly, New England (1894) p. 89.

64. Roger Kiska, "Antonio Gramsci's Long March Through History," *Religion and Liberty, vol. 29, no. 3*, Action Institute, (May 16, 2023).

65. Antonio Gramsci, "V. Fascist Reaction and Communist Strategy 1924-1926." In *A Gramsci Reader,* ed. David Forgacs (New York: Schocken, 1988), 160-180.

66. Huey P. Newton and Bobble Seale, The Black Panther, The Black Panthers' newspaper, May 15, 1967.

67. Yaron Steinbuch, New York Post, June 24, 2020. www.nypost.com/2020/06/25/blm-co-founder-describes-herself-as-trained-marxist

68. https://www.britannica.com/topic/propaganda.

69. Edward L. Bernays, *Propaganda*. London: Kennikat Press, 1928.

70. Joseph Goebbels, Speech addressing party supporters, Berlin, 1923.

71. Vladimir Lenin, a 1903 quote found in Eastman, "Reflections on the Failure of Socialism" (1955).

72. Joseph Stalin, Speech at the Twelfth Congress of the Russian Communist Party, April 19, 1923.

73. Alexander Solzhenitsyn, "A World Split Apart", Commencement Address, Harvard University, June 8, 1978.

74. Sonoma State Star, November 16, 2020.

75. Ibid.

76. Joost Meerloo, *The Rape of the Mind: The Psychology of Thought Control, Menticide, and Brain-washing*, 1956.

77. Samuel Adams, *letter to John Pitts in 1776*.

78. John Adams, *letter to J. H. Tiffany*, Mar. 31, 1819.

79. Theodore Dalrymple, *Our Future, What's Left of It*, Frontpage Magazine, (August 31, 2005).

80. Vladimir Lenin, Quoted in New York Times, December 26, 1955.

81. Elena Gorokhova, *A Mountain of Crumbs: A Memoir* (New York: Simon & Schuster) 2011, p. 172.

82. Adolph Hitler, *Mein Kampf*, vol. I, ch. X (1925).

83. Joost Meerloo, *The Rape of the Mind: The Psychology of Thought Control, Menticide, and Brainwashing*, 1956. 28.

84. Ibid.

85. Karl Marx to Joseph Wedemeyer, March 5, 1852, Marx, *Selected Works*, Co-Operative Publishing Society, Moscow, 1935, I, p. 377, As quoted in *The Naked Socialist* by Paul. B. Skousen (2014) p. 121.

86. Karl Marx, *A Contribution to the Critique of Hegel's Philosophy of Right*, 1844.

87. Karl Marx, *The Communist Manifesto*, Ch. 2 (1848).

88. Karl Marx, *Selected Essays*, The Floating Press, (2012) p. 75.

89. Bruce Deitrick Price, "Lenin's Train Goes Chugging Through American Education," The American Thinker, April 9, 2020.

90. Vladimir Lenin, as quoted in *The Proletarian Revolution and the Renegade Kautsky* (1972), p.11.

91. Vladimir Lenin, State and Revolution, (1919) chapter 4.

92. "Lenin's Hanging Order" (11 August 1918), an order for the execution of kulaks, as translated in *The Unknown Lenin: From the Secret Archive* (1996) by Richard Pipes, p. 50.

93. Joseph Stalin, said in 1923; Boris Bazhanov, *The Memoirs of Stalin's Former Secretary* (1992).

94. Joseph Stalin, Statement by a teenaged Stalin after reading The Origin of Species by Charles Darwin, Quoted in Simon Sebag Montefiore, *Young Stalin*, 2007.

95. Joseph Stalin, Interview with H. G. Wells, [New York, New Century Publishers, September 1937; reprinted October 1950. Joseph Stalin and H. G. Wells, Marxism VS. Liberalism: An Interview.]

96. Mao Zedong, "Interview with Three Correspondents from the Central News Agency, the Sao Tang Pao and the Hsin Min Pao" (September 16, 1939), Selected Works, Vol. II, p. 272.

97. "Women Have Gone to the Labour Front" (1955). *The Socialist Upsurge in China's Countryside,* Chinese ed., Vol. 1.

98. Frank Dikotter, *Mao's Great Famine: The History of China's Most Devastating Catastrophe, 1958-62, 2010.*

99. Mao Zedong, "Report on an Investigation of the Peasant Movement in Hunan" (March 1927) Selected Works, Vol. I, p.28

100. Mao Zedong, "Problems of War and Strategy" (November 6, 1938), Selected Works Vol. II.

101. Mao Zedong, Speech, "On the People's Democratic Dictatorship" (June 30, 1949). Selected Works, Vol. IV, p. 412.

102. *The Road to Serfdom*, F. A. Hayek, 50th-anniversary edition, The University of Chicago Press, (1994) footnote 9, p.35.

103. Adolph Hitler, *Mein Kampf* (1933), vol. I, ch. 6.

104. Ibid.

105. Ibid.

106. Ibid.

107. Joseph Goebbels, Diary, March 14, 1943, As quoted in *Eigen's Political and Historical Quotations.*

108. Ibid.

109. Fidel Castro, Quoted in Military Quotes/Quotations.

110. Fidel Castro, Speech, Havana, January 1961.

111. Fidel Castro, Speech on the anniversary of the Granma landing, December 2, 1961.

112. Isaiah 14:12-15, King James Version.

113. Karl Marx, (cited from Richard Wurmbrand, Marx and Satan, p. 12.)

114. Ludwig von Mises, *Human Action: A Treatise on Economics,* Martino Press, 1998.

115. Billy Graham, "We Need Revival," *Revival in our time: the story of the Billy Graham evangelistic campaigns, including six of his sermons*, (1950) Van Kampen Press.

116. John Dewey, "Soul-Searching," Teacher Magazine, September 1933, p. 33.

117. Psalm 119:130, King James Version.

118. John 8:31-32. King James Version.

119. Henry H. Halley. *Halley's Bible Handbook* (Grand Rapids, MI: Regency Reference Library, 1962), 19.

120. John Calvin Coolidge, 1923, statement. Charles Fadiman, ed. "The American Treasury" (NY: Harper & Brothers Publishers, 1955), p 127.

121. Karl Marx, Chapter 2. *The Manifesto of the Communist Party* (1848).

122. Karl Marx, *Karl Marx, Friedrich Engels, Vladimir Il'ich Lenin, Joseph Stalin (1948)*. "Ten Classics of Marxism".

123. Noah Webster, "On the Education of Youth in America" 1788.

124. Adolph Hitler, speech September 15, 1935.

125. Adolph Hitler, Speech, 6 Nov. 1933. Quoted in: William L. Shirer, *The Rise and Fall of The Third Reich,* 1959).

126. Dr. Chester M. Pierce, Harvard University, Keynote address to the Association for Childhood Education International, Denver, Colorado, April 1972, as quoted in numerous publications, such as Eakman, *op. cit.,* P. 369.

127. Noah Webster, *American Dictionary of the English Language*, 1828.

128. Ibid.

129. Ibid.

130. Martin Luther, To the Christian Nobility of the German States (1520), translated by Charles M. Jacobs, reported in rev. James Atkinson, The Christian in Society, I (Luther's Works, ed. James Atkinson, vol. 44), p. 207 (1966).

131. Thomas Jefferson to James Madison, December 20, 1787.

132. Dwight D. Eisenhower, Speech at William and Mary College, Williamsburg, Virginia, May 15, 1953.

133. James Madison to W. T. Barry, August 4, 1822.

134. James Madison to George Thompson, 1825.

135. Benjamin Rush, "On the Mode of Education Proper in a Republic," 1806.

136. Karl Marx, *The Communist Manifesto.*

137. Joseph Stalin, Interview with H. G. Wells, September 1937, *Eigen's Political and Historical Quotations.*

138. John Dewey, *The Later Works*, 1925-1953 (ed. Siu Press, 1989).

139. Benjamin Rush, *The Selected Writings of Benjamin Rush,* On Education, 114.

140. Noah Webster, *A Manual of Useful Studies: For the Instruction of Young Persons of Both Sexes, in Families and Schools*, New Haven: S. Babcock, 1839.

141. Karl Marx, *The Communist Manifesto*, ch. 2 (1848).

142. Ibid.

143. U.S. Const. amend. I.

144. George Washington, Address Delivered in Newburgh, New York on 15 March 1783.

145. Benjamin Franklin, letter from "Silence Dogood," no. 8, printed in *The New-England Courant,* Boston, Massachusetts, July 9, 1722.

146. Ibid.

147. Benjamin Franklin, "On Freedom of Speech and the Press," *The Pennsylvania Gazette,* Nov. 1737.

148. John Dewey, As quoted in Indoctrination: *How 'Useful Idiots' Are Using Our Schools to Subvert American Exceptionalism*, by Kyle Olson (2011), p. 129.

149. Herbert Marcuse, "Repressive Tolerance." In *A Critique of Pure Tolerance,* by Herbert Marcuse, 81-117, (Boston: Beacon Press), 1969.

150. Daniel Webster, *The Speeches of Daniel Webster*. Edited by B. F. Tefft. New York: Lincoln Centenary, 1907.

151. "From George Washington to the United Baptist Churches of Virginia, May 1789," *Founders Online,* National Archives.

152. "From George Washington to the Society of Quakers, 13 October 1789," *Founders Online*, National Archives.

153. Ronald Reagan's "Evil Empire Speech" to the National Association of Evangelicals, Orlando, FL, March 8, 1983.

154. Ronald Reagan's Address Before a Joint Session of the Alabama State Legislature in Montgomery, AL, March 15, 1982.

155. Vladimir Lenin, Socialism and Religion, 1905.

156. Noah Webster, "Advice to the Young," *History of the United States*, (New Haven: Durrie & Peck, 1832), 338-340.

157. Benjamin Rush (1806). "*Essays, Literary, Moral and Philosophical ...*", p.112.

158. Benjamin Rush, *Essays, Literary, Moral & Philosophical* (Philadelphia: Thomas & Samuel F. Bradford, 1798), pp. 94, 100, "A Defence of the Use of the Bible as a School Book."

159. Benjamin Rush, *Letters of Benjamin Rush*, L. H. Butterfield, editor (Princeton, NJ: Princeton University Press, 1951), Vol. I, p. 521, to Jeremy Belknap on July 13, 1789.

160. Daniel Webster, "The Voices of America's Heritage," Torch (Dallas, TX: Texas Eagle Forum, February 1994), vol. 1, no. 7, p. 4.

161. 1 Corinthians 1:18-21, King James Version.

162. 1 Corinthians 1:27-29, King James Version.

163. Galatians 4:4-7, ESV

164. Noah Webster, Preface to *American Dictionary of the English Language,* republished 1841.

165. George Washington, *The Writings of George Washington*, John C. Fitzpatrick, editor (Washington, D. C.: U. S. Government Printing Office, 1934), Vol. 11, pp. 342-343, General Orders of May 2, 1778.

166. Thomas Jefferson, Letter to Dr. Benjamin Rush, April 21, 1803.

167. Joseph Goebbels, Diary Excerpts, 16 October 1928.

168. Dr. Timothy Dwight, Cited by Christopher J. Klicka, *The Right Choice* (Gresham, OR: Noble, 1995), p. 90.

169. Daniel Webster, *Fourth of July Oration Delivered at Fryeburg, ME, in the Year 1802* (A. Williams & Co. / A.F. & C.W. Lewis, Boston, Mass. / Fryeburg, Me., 1882), 12.

170. Daniel Webster, *Fourth of July Oration Delivered at Hanover, NH*, in 1800.

171. Samuel Adams, *"The Writings of Samuel Adams: 1770-1773"*. P. 336.

172. Samuel Adams (Letter to James Warren, February 12, 1779)

173. Samuel Adams (Letter to James Warren, November 4, 1775)

174. Samuel Adams (1968). "The Writings of Samuel Adams: 1773-1777."

175. Vladimir Lenin, "The Tasks of the Youth Leagues" (October 7, 1920).

176. Ronald Reagan, "Evil Empire Speech" (8 March 1983).

177. Thomas Jefferson, Declaration and Protest of Virginia, (1825). ME 17:445.

178. "John Adams to Abigail Adams, 7 July 1775."

179. Abraham Lincoln, Speech, Kalamazoo, MI, August 27, 1856, *Eigen's Political and Historical Quotations.*

180. Abraham Lincoln, Notes for Speeches at Columbus and Cincinnati, September 16 and 17, 1859.

181. Daniel Webster, The earliest version of this seems to be from *Savings and Loan Annual 1963*, p. 56, published by the United States Savings and Loan League.

182. James Madison, Speech in the Virginia constitutional convention, Richmond, Virginia, December 2, 1829.

183. James Madison's notes on the debates in the Federal Convention, avalon.law.yale.edu. July 11, 1787.

184. James Madison, On Tyranny, Federalist Paper #47.

185. Alexander Hamilton (1851). *"The Works of Alexander Hamilton: Comprising His* Correspondence, *and His Political and Official Writings, Exclusive of the Federalist, Civil and Military. Published from the Original Manuscripts Deposited in the Department of State, by Order of the Joint Library Committee of Congress", p.164.*

186. Vladimir Lenin, As quoted in *The Proletarian Revolution and the Renegade Kautsky* (1972), p. 11.

187. Vladimir Lenin, Speech to the 7th Congress of CPSU (b), March 8, 1918, Selected Works (International Publishers, New York, 1943), vol. viii, p. 222.

188. Adolph Hitler, paraphrased from Mein Kampf, Manheim trans., p. 720.

189. James Madison, I Annals of Congress 434 [June 8, 1789].

190. U.S. Const. amend II.

191. Samuel Adams, ("The Rights of the Colonists," November 20, 1772).

192. George Mason, referencing advice given to the British Parliament by Pennsylvania governor Sir William Keith, *The Debates in the Several State Conventions on the Adoption of the Federal Constitution*, June 14, 1788.

193. Noah Webster, An Examination of the Leading Principles of the Federal Constitution, October 10, 1787.

194. Mao Zedong, *Selected Works of Mao Tse-tung* (1965), vol. II, p. 224.

195. Joseph Stalin, The Political Report of the Central Committee, The Fifteenth Congress, December 7, 1927.

196. John Maynard Keynes. *The Economic Consequences of The Peace*, vol. 2 (London: Macmillan) 1919, VI 13.

197. Ayn Rand, "Who Will Protect Us from Our Protectors?" *The Objectivist Newsletter,* May 1962, 18.

198. Ludwig von Mises, *The Theory of Money and Credit,* p. 436.

199. Calvin Coolidge, "Inaugural Address," on March 4, 1925. *As found in The Mind of the President.*

200. Thomas Jefferson to John Taylor, 1816. ME 15:23.

201. Thomas Jefferson, Declaration and Protest of Virginia, 1825. ME 17:445.

202. Vladimir Lenin, quoted in Michael White and Kurt Schuler, "Unveiled! Lenin's Brilliant Plot to Destroy Capitalism," *The Atlantic,* Sept. 26, 2013.

203. Joseph Goebbels, https://slate.com/news-and-politics/2017/03/how-nazi-propaganda-encouraged-the-masses-to-co-produce-a-false-reality.html.

204. Victor Davis Hanson, "Obama: Transforming America", National Review, October 1, 2013. https://www.nationalreview.com/2013/10/obama-transforming-america-victor-davis-hanson/

205. Ibid.

206. Karl Marx, Friedrich Engels, (1978) *Karl Marx, Friedrich Engels: Collected Works.* Russia: International Publishers, vo.10, p. 281.

207. Vladimir Lenin, *State and Revolution* (1919) ch. 4.

208. Karl Marx, *The Communist Manifesto,* ch. 2.

209. James Madison, speech in the House of Representatives, January 10, 1794.

210. U.S. Const., preamble.

211. James Madison: Annals of Congress 179 (1794).

212. Samuel Adams, from a letter written by Adams in the name of the Massachusetts House of Representatives to Dennys de Berdt, 12 January 1768.

213. Frédéric Bastiat, Economic sophisms, 2nd series (1848), ch. 1 Physiology of plunder ("Sophismes économiques", 2ème série (1848), chap. 1 "Physiologie de la spoliation"). - Economic Sophisms (1845-1848).

214. Frédéric Bastiat, *The Law* (1850).

215. Matthew 7:15, King James Version.

216. Galatians 1:6-8,10-12, King James Version.

217. Karl Marx, "Critique of the Gotha Programme," pt. 1 (1875).

218. Joseph Stalin, Anarchism or Socialism (1906).

219. Winston Churchill, Speech in the House of Commons, (1948).

220. Joseph Stalin, Interview Between J. Stalin and Roy Howard (March 1, 1936).

221. Karl Marx, *"Selected Essays,"* p.75, *The Floating Press* (2012).

222. Vladimir Lenin, The State and Revolution, 5.

223. Samuel Adams, addressing a meeting of delegates to the Continental Congress, assembled at Yorktown, Pennsylvania, September 1777; as quoted

in The Life and Public Services of Samuel Adams, Volume 2, by William Vincent Wells; Little, Brown, and Company; Boston, 1865; pp. 492-493.

224. George Washington, "General Orders, 2 July 1776."

225. Benjamin Franklin, debates in the Constitutional Convention, Philadelphia, Pennsylvania, June 28, 1787. James Madison, *Journal of the Federal Convention,* ed. E. H. Scott, pp. 259-60 (1893).

226. James Madison, As quoted in The Federalist (Philadelphia: Benjamin Warner, 1818), p. 194, James Madison, Federalist #37. 1788.

227. Patrick Henry, The "Give Me Liberty or Give Me Death" Speech, 1775. https://www.historicstjohnschurch.org/the-speech

228. Patrick Henry, Letter to Archibald Blair, January 8, 1799, in William Wirt Henry, *Patrick Henry: Life, Correspondence, and Speeches, 1891, Vol 2:592.*

229. Ephesians 6:14-17, CEV.

230. Henry H. Halley. *Halley's Bible Handbook* (Grand Rapids, MI: Regency Reference Library, 1962), 19.

231. Noah Webster, *History of the United States* (New Haven: Durrie and Peck, 1832) p. 300, Sec. 578.

232. John 8:31-32, King James Version.

233. Maximilien Robespierre, As quoted in *Human Rights and Freedoms in the USSR* (1981) by Fedor Eliseevich Medvedev and Gennadiĭ Ivanovich Kulikov, p. 221.

234. John Adams, In Defense of the British Soldiers on trial for the Boston Massacre, December 4, 1770.

235. George Washington, Letter to Charles M. Thruston, August 10, 1794.

236. Vladimir Lenin, a 1903 quote found in Eastman, "Reflections on the Failure of Socialism" (1955).

237. Hebrews 11:6, King James Version.

238. 2 Chronicles 16:9, Holy Bible: Contemporary English Version. (1995). New York: American Bible Society.

239. Psalm 81:13-14, King James Version.

240. 1 Chronicles 5:20, NCV.

241. Abraham Lincoln, Farewell Address, Springfield, IL (February 11,1861.

242. Deuteronomy 6:25, King James Version.

243. Psalm 18:24, NCV.

244. 2 Corinthians 6:6-7, GNT.

245. Samuel Adams, addressing a meeting of delegates to the Continental Congress, assembled at Yorktown, Pennsylvania, September 1777; as quoted in The Life and Public Services of Samuel Adams, Volume 2, by William Vincent Wells; Little, Brown, and Company; Boston, 1865; pp. 492-493.

246. Franklin D. Roosevelt, D-Day Prayer. June 6, 1944. https://www.presidency.uscb.edu/documents/prayer-d-day

247. James 5:16, King James Version.

248. Philippians 4:6-7, King James Version.

249. Psalm 34:15-16, CEV.

250. Chronicles 7:14, King James Version.

251. Ephesians 4:11-13, NCV.

252. Ephesians 4:14-16, NCV.

253. Ronald Reagan, Remarks to the Annual Convention of the Concerned Women of America, September 25, 1987.

254. Ronald Reagan, Remarks at the National Conference of the Building and Construction Trades Department, AFL-CIO, March 30, 1981.

255. Ronald Reagan, Farewell Address to the Nation, January 11, 1989.

256. Ronald Reagan, A Time for Choosing Speech, October 27, 1964.

257. Thomas Jefferson, Letter to Charles Yancey, 6 Jan. 1816.

258. "From Thomas Jefferson to Richard Price, 8 January 1789."

259. "From Thomas Jefferson to Edward Carrington, 16 January 1787."

260. Ephesians 4:17-19, NCV.

261. Ibid. verses 20-24.

262. Ibid. verses 25-28.

263. Ibid. verses 29-32.

www.ingramcontent.com/pod-product-compliance
Lightning Source LLC
Chambersburg PA
CBHW030336010526
44119CB00047B/520